The Forgetting of Being

The Forgetting of Being

Peter Paz

Library of Congress Control Number: 2007902412
ISBN: Hardcover   978-1-4257-7992-4
                 Softcover   978-1-4257-7984-9

This book was printed in the United States of America.

To order additional copies of this book, contact:
Xlibris Corporation
1-888-795-4274
www.Xlibris.com
Orders@Xlibris.com
38911

CONTENTS

PART I
ISRAEL—NEW YORK 1945-1990

PART II
NICE: 1990-2001

Dedicated to

Joe Katz, my analyst

Much of my journal, I am afraid, is bleak and politically out of step with the times and may be upsetting to you. If so, I'm truly sorry. On the other hand, I feel that were it not for you, I would still be in hiding. I would certainly never have been able to write this.

ABOUT THE AUTHOR

Peter Paz was born Peter Sigmund Goldmann in Berlin 1937. As a child, he was interned in a concentration camp and liberated at the end of the war when he was eight years old. He was sent as an orphan to a displaced persons' camp in Marseille, France, and then to the Kibbutz Afek in Israel, where his name was changed to Yigal Paz.

After his military service In Israel, he studied dance with Anna Sokolov, touring Israel and New York with her company. In 1963, Peter won a full scholarship to The Julliard School of Music in New York. He continued his training with Martha Graham and returned to Israel to perform with the Batsheba Dance Theater.

He eventually left dance to pursue a photography career in New York. After working in news and film, he became an established international corporate photographer, working for clients who included Exxon, BP, McCormick, Otis, and Aerospatial, among others.

He was married to and divorced from Luba Paz, with whom he had a daughter, Lyrissa.

In 1990, he moved from New York to France with Beverly Pimsleur, his companion for the last twenty years of his life. He died, after a long illness, on October 2l, 2001, in Nice.

EDITOR'S NOTE

Peter was a familiar sight in the cafés of the port of Nice. With his signature Australian hat and his laptop, he followed the sun: the Port Café or Cappa in the morning, under the arches in the afternoon where the last rays streamed across the Place Garibaldi. To questions of "What are you writing?" he answered with an ironic and enigmatic smile, "My memoirs."

He always intended to finish working on them, to put them "in order," but sadly, his illness and subsequent death intervened and he left the manuscript incomplete. Faced with the multiple versions of each chapter, some left unfinished, I had to make many arbitrary decisions, about the "order,"—what to include and what to leave out. I am sure that Peter would have had his own ideas about how to construct the book; in his absence I have tried to follow the few directives he left and, above all, to be true to his "voice," leaving in his idiosyncrasies of speech and style, so uniquely his.

Even though some of the subject matter of *Forgetting of Being* is painful, Peter's optimism, humor, and gentle humanity shine through. His writing style is original, strong, and poetic, influenced by his multilingual background. The result is an unusual and very different sort of survivor memoir.

A more understanding man there never was, so I think he would accept that choices had to be made in shaping his memoirs, even if they were not his own. But it was the only way to give them life and, by doing so, prolong his.

Beverly Pimsleur
New York, 2005

"We who survived the camps are not true witnesses. It is an uncomfortable notion, which I have gradually come to accept by reading what other survivors have written, including myself, when I reread my writing after a lapse of years. We, the survivors, are not only a tiny, but also an anomalous minority. We are those who, through prevarications, skill and luck, never touched bottom. Those who have, and who have seen the face of the Gorgon, did not return or returned wordless."

—Primo Levi

At first I thought, I should start this story from the end. It made more sense that way. By saying sense, I mean it made some sense. Coming from the beginning, this story wouldn't add up—it's a disaster. Of course, I know that starting at the beginning is the rule, and many books are full of why it makes good sense. But life, at least this life, is not about rules, or reason or sense.

Peter Paz,
Nice, 1991

PART I

Israel—New York
1945-1990

PROLOGUE

France, July 1987

We celebrated our 50th birthdays under the light of the setting sun on the terrace of the restaurant Les Beaux de Provence. Riding the last waves of the perfumed breeze of summer, high on the air, and the wine, feeling mellow, I told Beverly that I finally felt at peace with myself and the world.

Claude Lanzmann's nine-hour documentary film, *Shoah,* was playing at the Coliseum Cinema in New York when we came back from our month in France. It was a retelling of how it was done: the portrayal of the methodical destruction of Europe's Jews and gypsies as recounted by its victims, perpetrators, collaborators, and witnesses. It left me numb. It was a part of my past, yet so remote it no longer had much to do with my life, I felt. As my analyst used to say: "That was then and now is now." But weeks later the ghostlike characters of Lanzmann's film returned to haunt me. First was the man sitting at the nose of the boat gliding on the tranquil waters of Treblinka, recounting his daily routine of loading the bodies into the ovens (the images swimming in my head as I was swimming laps at my club in Grand Central). A burned-out lightbulb in my mind had suddenly come to life, moving at random from chamber to chamber, projecting images on walls that had been dark all these years. As the light came on, there was the barber in his Tel Aviv barbershop, recounting cutting the hair of the people of his own village, including his wife's, before they entered the gas chamber. The commandant of Treblinka talking about maintaining his quota against all logic and human nature, the Polish aristocrat recounting his journey to tell the outside world about what was happening to the Jews of Warsaw and how the leaders of New York's Jewish community chose not to believe his story and turned him away. The images would appear, linger, fade away, and then reappear.

A few weeks later, the children of the stones, born in the ghettos of Palestine, rose to reclaim their future from "the children of the dream."* It was no surprise, but when I saw the first TV images showing Jewish soldiers shooting Palestinian children armed with stones, I found it hard to bring myself to believe it was actually taking place. As the images became routine, the feeling that it had all been foretold, inevitable, began to sink in, boosting me out of the orbit in which I had been circling steadily since Russian troops liberated my camp in 1945.

---

*   reference to the first Intifada, 1987

CHAPTER 1

THE KIBBUTZ BY THE SEA

Israel, 1945

Not a soul at the displaced persons camp mentioned the Palestinians in Palestine. Palestine was for the Jews. Period. So it was a big surprise to see them one morning on the other side of our kibbutz fence, dark little figures in the dunes. We watched them through the barbed wire, moving in step with their goats and their dogs, to the sound of the bells, inching their way in the tall grass, from one blade to the next, gathering snails.

One day they approached the fence, hesitantly. We started talking. There was much giggling all around. They were interested in the girls: "Show us yours and we will show you ours," they said. When the girls refused, they pulled out theirs and pissed at us through the fence. Not wanting to be outdone, we pulled ours out and pissed back at them. We continued to meet this way off and on, with minor variations in the scenario. In time, our meetings became less frequent, because the smell of the place became more powerful than the thrill of the game.

Then, some weeks later, rifle shots rang throughout the morning class. At break time, we rushed out. Less then a hundred meters from the schoolhouse, we came upon a pile of dead dogs. I remember standing there, looking at the dead dogs, stupefied when Nurit started yelling: "It's Gilli, my Gilliiii, Gilliiiii, Gilliiiiiiiii."

We never did find out how Gilli ended up being shot dead that morning, along with the dogs belonging to the Palestinian shepherds. I do remember my classmates being upset about Gilli. But we never talked about it: "Gilli was dead," they said. "What was the point?" The Palestinian shepherds never came to the fence again. I was eight and a half then. Peter and I had just arrived from Germany at the Kibbutz by the Sea. It all of a sudden seemed like yesterday.

PETER*

Israel, 1945

He was tall, transparently thin, with mournful dark eyes hopelessly crossed. He used to run into things, twitter, stumble around, and finally crash into one thing or another. It made everyone laugh. It never failed. The more we laughed, the more he did it, the more he did it, the better he got at it, the better he got, the more attention he drew to himself. At the beginning, there was talk about an operation to fix his eyes, but he incurred the wrath of our teacher, to whom his act was anything but a cause for laughter, so much so that he was expelled before the operation was done. As I look at him from the distance of time, his image stands like a Giacometti's Don Quixote against the horizon. The longer I look, the taller he is.

The boat to Israel, 1945

He was sitting by my side holding on to the railings, feet dangling overboard. The boat was slowly gliding into port, toward a curtain of lights hanging from a tall sky. Out there in the dark is our paradise, I thought. In the games we played at the camp for displaced persons in Marseille, everyone wanted to be an American soldier. Most everyone I met said they were waiting to go to America. When I was told that I would not be sent to America, I was crushed. To console me, I was told that Palestine is our "promised land," the Land of the Jews, and that only the luckiest people get to go there. "In Palestine, you will be free, money grows on trees, you will never have to worry about anything; it is our paradise."

So when on that spring night I was sitting on the deck of a boat, crowded with refugees gazing at the lights of Haifa, I was shivering more out of excitement and anticipation of setting foot in "paradise" than from the chill in the breeze. I fell asleep on deck, transfixed by the shifting lights of the city, reflected in the water below, and the steady sound of the waves lapping at the side of the boat. It was early evening the next day when we were finally allowed off the boat. The people of Haifa were at the dock to greet us with oranges, sandwiches, bananas, and songs. It was like walking into a dream.

---

*   not to be confused with writer of this memoir, whose name is also Peter

The holding camp, near Haifa, 1945

On the bus, I took the orange out of the bag, rolled it in my hands, smelled it, and bit into it. It had a bitter taste. I noticed Peter sniffing a banana and asked if he would trade: "My orange for your sandwich?" He gave me a look: one eye said yes, the other said no, and the rest of his face said, "Hey, what kind of a fool do you take me for? I will take your sandwiches for my banana!" And that was that. I went back to my sandwich, chewing in silence, looking out the window.

The old bus coughing its way up the mountain passed barbed-wire fences, watchtowers, searchlights, the works. A cold chill was crawling up my spine: "There are camps out there." Peter was leaning over now, mouth open, frozen in midchew, eyes glued to the window, unblinking. It was the searchlights illuminating the bus from both sides that made me realize the floor was yellow with peels of bananas and oranges.

"Everyone will be leaving in a few days. In the meantime, you are free to come and go as you like," it was announced to us over the loud speaker.

We walked out through the gate as soon as breakfast was over. There was nothing around but shrubs and nettle trees. Down below lay the city and the sea. We started cautiously on our way down the slope, slowly picking up speed, letting ourselves go. Soon we were riding in a blur on the seat of our pants, howling in delight, down the mountain. Wandering around the port district, we came upon a stadium. It was a rinky-dink thing, fenced all around with rusty corrugated tin construction sheets. We let ourselves in through one of the many loose corners. Inside it was half-time. Everyone was shouting, waving their hands. A little man strapped to a big box was running back and forth, furiously handing out colored things on a stick. Just like they told us in Marseille, I thought. I was in paradise, no question about it. I raised a hand with two fingers, and there he was in a flash, a hand stretched out with two popsicles. I was halfway down my popsicle when I noticed him out of the corner of my eye, standing there, staring at me with an all too familiar glint of expectation in his eyes. It was unmistakable. He was actually after money, which was a big surprise, given that "in Palestine," they kept saying, "Money grew on trees." Quickly we ducked, slid down under the benches, and took off, popsicles dripping in hand, through our hole in the fence. I really believed the stuff about money in the trees. It took some time before I got over feeling stupid for believing it.

"A truck will be coming for you tomorrow after breakfast," we were told. "You are going to a kibbutz." I had no idea where or what a "kibbutz" was, but I asked no questions, neither did Peter. We had nowhere else to go. All we had to do was be there when they called out our names and get on the truck.

It was a delivery truck covered by a pink tarpaulin. We settled in the back corners, watching the scenery pull away, rolling along with the morning traffic. Sometime later, the truck slowed down, turned off the main road, and after a short bumpy ride, it stopped. A few one-story gray wooden buildings, unconnected by road or sidewalk and perched on blocks of stone, were scattered in the dunes, like a train derailed in a desert. Tall grass was growing in patches around, between and under the buildings. In the distance, under a bright sun, a group of children were standing still, looking at us.

The driver brought us to the wrong place was my first thought. It must be a mistake; this couldn't possibly be the place where only the luckiest of people get to go to. The place they told me about at the transit camp in Marseille where you will be free, never have to fear, or worry about a thing: "It is our paradise!" I repeated it to myself over and over, sitting on that truck, looking out at the scene of desolation ringed by barbed wire.

In broken German and a polite smile, the driver urged us to get off his truck. I ignored him, pretending not to understand, and retreated into my corner. Seeing that we were not getting off, the children came over. After they exchanged a few words with our driver, he dropped the smile and became insistent, stamping his feet in the sand and flailing his arms in the air, ordering us to get off. When that failed, he charged the truck and climbed on with a groan. At which point, Peter and I jumped off.

We followed the children to an isolated stone building near the barbed-wire fence: the children's house. Waiting for us at the door, in a white apron, was the metapelet*. She showed us to the shower room and in perfect German ordered us to undress. Surprised, I stared at her, making no move toward undressing. Neither did Peter. After a few minutes of silence, she went in to a long lecture about having to clean us up before lunch and having no time to play games. Though she was good-natured about it, my impression was that there was no getting past her. I undressed.

She brought out a pair of scissors and unceremoniously began cutting my hair. While it was sliding down my face, I could see Peter's emaciated legs, his hands folded over his privates, waiting his turn. I watched him being sheared

---

* The person on the Kibbutz, usually a woman, who took care of the children when they were not in the classroom.

from the warm shower. When she was done with him, it was my turn again. She opened a big can of black ointment, dipped her hand in, and began smearing the stuff on me, from my bald head all the way down to my toes. It had a sickening foul smell. "Wait here," she said when she was done.

She went on to smear the black ointment on Peter with great care, making sure there were no bald spots. I was mesmerized by the scene, could not take my eyes off them. When she was finished with him, he looked like a burned corpse standing up. "I will put these in the fire," she said, gathering our clothes. "I will be back in a minute with proper clothes!" She was out the door.

Finally, we were ready, presentable. There was a small mirror hanging over a sink. I looking at it, trying to make up my mind. Do I want to see what I looked like before being presented or not? It was a shock seeing myself: I was gone. The only thing left of me were my eyes and lips. I looked like Peter.

We were led into the dining room; a woman was waiting for us. "My name is Esther Katzenelson," she said, smiling a thin wooden smile. "I am your teacher, and this is your new home." We were seated at the opposite ends of a long dining table, like birthday boys. Without hair, the top of my head was cold, as if it was open. I smelled of death.

"This," she declared, pointing at me, smiling, "is Peter. And this"—pointing at Peter—"is also Peter. They have just arrived 'from over there.'" She said this while still smiling, translating to us.

"Peter is a German name!" she declared, again smiling. "Now that you are in Palestine, you must have proper Hebrew names." She renamed us on the spot! Peter became *Yiftach*. "He who shall open the gates of Palestine,'" she said, pointing at him with an inexplicable sense of self-pride. While I was still wondering why she was smiling, I became *Yigal*. "He who shall redeem the arriving multitudes." She ended our introduction by telling the children: "They have suffered much and should be left to do as they please."

Even though I understood her words, it all seemed like a dream. I understood nothing: What did she mean by "suffered much"? What was wrong with my real name? Across the table, Peter seemed lost; his eyes were in a grotesquely fixed position, looking everywhere and nowhere at the same time.

Between the smell coming off my body and the smell of the beans on my plate, I felt sick: *What will happen if I throw up here on the plate*, I wondered. *Or should I get up, leave the table?* Afraid to draw the teacher's attention to myself, I stayed, hoping I would not throw up before she was finished.

It was nap time—mandatory—enforced by the metapelet, who went from room to room, back and forth, ordering everyone by name: "Stop talking, turn to the wall," until the building was quiet. Peter and I were exempt. *It would be a good time to check the place out*, I thought and went to fetch Peter. He was lying awake, on his back on white sheets, staring at the ceiling. His roommates were asleep, facing the wall.

There were five small bedrooms connected by a long corridor. At the end was a large dining room, two toilets, and the shower room in which there were cubicles: twenty-two open cubicles, each with a sticker and a name. In addition to clothes and personal knickknacks, there were little paper bags with nuts, candies, raisins, fresh dates, and dried figs. We went from cubicle to cubicle, gathered the bags, and emptied everything in a big pile on the floor.

Just as we were about to start feasting on the stuff, one of the children appeared at the door. Within seconds, they all came running through the door, quickly forming a tight circle around us. There was nothing for us to do but wait. I kept looking up at the ring of eyes looking down at us while they went on about what to do, back and forth. There was something curious in those eyes, something in the way they looked at us made me think of the smiling teacher saying: "They have suffered much . . . they should be left alone, to do as they please . . ."

Realizing that they were not going to move on us, we started eating, hesitantly at first, conscious of their presence. But we soon forgot all about them, eating everything to the last raisin, leaving nothing but candy wrappers, nutshells, and marks of the black ointment on the gray tiled floor.

I dreaded the approaching evening meal. When it came and went without a word about our stealing their Passover candies being mentioned, I knew there was something wrong. In fact, the teacher turned to us in the middle of dinner saying something to the effect that "We want you to feel at home here," smiling the same smile she had on when she renamed us. "So my house will be your home." She pointed to me. "Any time you feel like it, you are welcome in my house." Peter, in turn, was assigned to the house of Otto Schnitzler, a reclusive middle-aged man, silenced by a severe speech impediment.

Something isn't right in this place, a voice in me kept whispering. Sooner or later the cubicle episode will be brought up. We will be punished. I was certain of it. "Shit, shit, shit," Peter kept spitting under his breath as we wandered around in the tall weeds, like two ghostly shadows, looking for a place to talk, to be alone.

Not far behind the children's house, we came upon a mini-animal farm: pigeons, rabbits in cages, a goat, chickens, and roosters walking about behind a meshed-wire fence. As soon as we were inside the fence, he started all over again: "Shit, shit, bloody damned shiiettt," kicking everything in sight, chasing the chickens up in the air. "This place is a shiiiiiit, damned shiiiiiit. This teacher must be crazy, to call this place home. It is a camp!" he said, when we finally sat down on an overturned feeding bucket. "I am not staying." Within a minute he was up again, chased by demons. Walking around moving his head like a chicken pecking the air: "This . . . is . . . your . . . home . . . this . . . is . . . your . . . home," over and over, squeezing each word out from a contorted, crooked smile.

"What do you want to do?"

"Get away! I don't care, right now!" he said.

In the evening, parents began arriving at the children's house. Not wanting to be seen, I quickly got into bed with my clothes on, pulled the sheet over my head, leaving myself a small slit through which I could breathe, and observed what was going on, while pretending I was asleep. A mother and a father were sitting on the edge of the bed opposite mine. On the bed in the corner, a mother was sitting reading from a book. I could hear others talking to their children in hushed soft tones. For a while, I watched them through the slit in the sheet, forgetting myself, slowly letting myself be carried away by the hushed soft voices.

It was the smell of the ointment that brought me back. I was hot. I felt nauseous; I needed more air. Controlling my breath became harder and harder, but I was determined not to come out from under the sheet. I didn't move. As my discomfort increased, I realized I was trapped. "How could you let yourself end up like this," I kept asking myself, over and over, "lying here like a black bug turned on its back." The anger was sucking me in. Tears came oozing out of my eyes, rolling down the side of my face. The ointment was burning my eyes. I squeezed them and squeezed them, shut tight as hard as I could, until I was no longer there.

"I am going!" Peter was whispering in my ear, shaking me. "Let's go!" The building was silent. We took some bread and leftovers from the dining room and quietly walked into the night. The back gate of the barbed-wire fence was unattended. We crossed over the railroad track, past the forest, and onto the beach. We walked at the edge of the water until we came to the end of the forest. We slept what was left of the night under a tree.

In the morning, we washed off the black ointment in the cool sea, tied our shoes to a stick, and followed the marks of the tide in the sand. Up ahead, hanging in the mist on the side of the mountain, was Haifa. It seemed strangely near.

It came out of nowhere, an armored personnel carrier racing toward us. The soldiers, already spread out, were closing in. It was too late to run. On

the truck, they gave us chewing gum and candy and drove us back to the
kibbutz. They waited patiently while we took forever putting our shoes on
and waved to us before taking off. Our classmates were there, watching us
from the distance.

We continued to run away but were returned each time by the soldiers.
Eventually we realized we had nowhere to run to and gave up.

The first time it happened was the morning after our first failed escape.
Halfway into the morning lesson, the teacher grabbed Peter by the collar,
pulled him out of his chair, dragged him to the center of the room, and was all
over him, like a cloud of angry bees in a Disney cartoon, beating and kicking
him, not letting up until he was curled up at her feet. Out of breath, face
flushed, large beads of perspiration hanging from her forehead and mustache,
she looked down at him, challenging him to get up so she could knock him
down all over again.

Leaning on his hands, he was looking around the room, not quite sitting
up, his mouth hanging open in surprise, like a dog that had been hit by a car.
There were no tears in his eyes, just bewilderment. His lips began moving;
he was trying to say something, but just as he was about to say it, they froze
in midsentence. He saw something in the faces, something that made him
realize what everyone knew, that there was no point in saying anything. So,
as his lips were moving on empty, his mind discovered a hole in the fence,
taking its first step out.

We had this guard in the camp who used to beat us. Seeing the teacher
standing over Peter, I saw him again: hose tucked under the stump of his
amputated arm, reaching for the head of his victim. Forcing it down between
his knees. Reaching for the hose and bringing his one arm down, mechanically,
one stroke at the time, repeatedly, slowly, taking his time, without a change
taking place in his face, as if he were a beating machine. As his beating became
a routine, I got used to the sight, and the shivers of fear that came on with it.
I continued to fear him, but one day I realized I no longer shivered.

With the palm of her hand, she wiped the sweat off her face and continued
the class, as though nothing had happened. Stunned by the ferocity of the
violence, I sat there paralyzed by fear, shivering: I was next. When she didn't
beat me, I was relieved, but I wondered: "Why did she beat him? What was
it all about? Did she beat him because we tried to escape?" I could not figure
it out and neither could Peter.

"It was nothing, it didn't really hurt," he said, when we were alone. But
the light in his eyes that was there when we slid down the mountain was gone.
He seemed deflated, like a balloon that has gone soft and lost its sheen.

By dinnertime, everyone knew every detail of how Peter had been beaten. Beating a child in the kibbutz was rare, but charging a member with beating a child was hot stuff. What made this case special was that our teacher was also the niece of a Zionist icon. On the other side was Peter, with no connections, no power. No one was likely to stand up for him, certainly not raise hell. Except for Otto Schnitzler, who most members dismissed even when they could not understand what he was saying.

He was so taken aback by the sight of Peter that evening that he kept pacing from wall to wall in his little room, speechless, making strange sounds, even though Peter sitting on his bed kept interjecting: "It was nothing, it did not really hurt."

For days afterward, Peter walked around the kibbutz black and pink all over. He did not think it strange—and at the time, neither did I—that not one person asked him "What happened to you? Who did this to you?"

JOE

New York, 1970s

"I can't imagine that no one spoke up for him," said Joe Katz, my New York analyst, looking out the window.

Peter: Why not?
Joe: Because it was inhuman.
P: Are you saying you would have?
J: I think so.
P: So would I, I hope. But it is easy for us, we live in New York, an openly Jewish city, a free society full of PTAs*.
J: Are you saying that the kibbutz is not free?
P: It depends on how you define being free: The members of the kibbutz were free from hunger, the roof over their heads was guaranteed, as was their children's education. But if you speak of the mind, or the spirit, it is not freer in the kibbutz than it was in the ghetto. There was in fact nothing free about life in the kibbutz. It is as ideologically rigid as are religious communes.
J: You can't be serious.

---

*   Parent Teachers Association

P: Do I shock you?

J: It sounds crazy!

P: It is crazy, that's why I am here. He did not respond.

J: Why do you think no one stood up for him?

P: There is no simple answer. Much of it has to do with the nature of the
       kibbutz. But most of it, I believe, has to do with Zionist doctrine.

J: What do you mean?

P: Imagine you are a passenger on a life-long cruise, on a boat that goes
       nowhere, docks nowhere. What would it take for you to pick a fight
       with a fellow passenger? Keep in mind that to get off, one must jump
       and swim, and you don't know how.

J: It would take a lot. I would certainly be careful.

P: That's what they were: careful. And there is the invisible fence. On a
       kibbutz, confrontations, on any issue, are best avoided. The question
       on many minds that evening was "What do I do about Peter? Do I
       speak up now? Do I raise hell? After all, my child could be next. Or
       should I wait until I cool off? Or best yet, wait until the Saturday night
       meeting when someone else may bring it up?" And then, a member has
       to carefully consider "Who am I up against? Who will join me in the
       ring, so to speak? Who will join my opponent?" And last but not least:
       "What will happen to my wife, my children, and my own position in
       the kibbutz if I lose?" These considerations must have been on many
       minds as they turned off the lights of that first night. In the end, it
       mattered little why they said nothing, did nothing when he walked
       by them the first time, bruised as he was. In averting their eyes, they
       rendered Peter invisible—fair game—a message that was not lost on
       our teacher.

J: What was Otto like?

P: He was a mensch.

OTTO

He made up the cereals, mixed the ingredients (including vitamins and
minerals) for all creatures that walked on all fours, plus chickens. "Mmmmmost
of this stuffffff . . . is alssso gooood foooooooooooooooor . . . you toooo . . ."
he'd say, as he brought up little packages of colorful powders, crushed grains,
nuts, and dried fruit from a sack. "SSSSSSmeeeeeeeeelllllll . . . it, ttttaaaste it,
ffffeeeeeeell it," he'd say and tell us all about it (in perfect German). What it
was, where it came from, why it was important. Then, like a magician, he'd

take a little bit of this and a little of that, mix it all up in a tin plate, make us sniff it, and guess which animal it was intended for. We never did get very good at guessing what it was, but we came to understand him, perfectly.

Otto's home was a room, a small room, dark and dingy, full of dust, the scent of cereals, socks, and body odor. He was a fountain of knowledge, from the most esoteric to the mundane. He had a small collection of records: mostly Mozart, some Bach, Haydn, Schubert, and a Stravinsky. He'd carefully wipe off the dust against the elbow of his shirt, put it on an old, hand-cranked phonograph, crank it up with a surgeon's precision, lay down the needle, and sit back to listen. His eyes would close, and as the music came on, his face would light up. He was gone, flying away in an infinite world all his own, and as if by magic, the whole room was alight.

Forever inventing new games, little plays, he took delight in amusing us—from chasing imaginary flies with any piece of clothing we could get our hands on, to chasing little and big mice that were all too real. And when our breath was gone, there were always stories. We'd sketch them out and play/act the characters, starting out on his bed in the center of the room as the stage, and then spilling out into the rest of the room, all free-flowing, on the wings of heavenly music.

By the time to go back to the children's house, we were mostly rolling around in tears of laughter, exhausted. The room around us looking like it was bombed. It was the brightest spot in the world. the one place I remember of my childhood that was filled with light and laughter.

On account of the war, I didn't start school on the kibbutz until I was nine. Needless to say, I had a lot of learning problems, but my most troublesome problem was the number 4. It seemed I just could not get my 4's to fit in anything. After a while of struggling with it, I just gave up, dropping number 4 altogether, excluding it from every question in which it appeared. Of course, I got all my arithmetic questions wrong, but since I was getting them wrong all along, it did not really worry me too much. What surprised and worried me was that my teacher was concerned: "Arithmetic is basic," she declared, giving me a long diagonal look, "life is chaos without it." I stared at her blankly, uncomprehending. I did a lot of that then. Chaos, I realized, must have been really scary to her. It was only natural then that she would think that it would frighten me too. It didn't: Life, as far as I could tell, was chaos. I could not imagine it any other way. In fact, I kind of liked it that way, still do. True, I felt stupid much of the time, getting every arithmetic problem wrong was no fun. But there were so many things wrong with me then, that one more didn't matter that much.

But my teacher had as much trouble with the term "giving up" as I had with the number 4. It was unfortunate because she couldn't keep me at the table, staring at number 4's as if they were a plate full of beans, not letting me go until the plate was clean, which she used to do when we had beans. There was not much she could do about my number 4 problem, and I knew it.

However, having seen her lose her temper, I knew I had to be careful. I was scared of her and kind of retreated into myself, floating in a milky nothingness, away from her voice, pounding out the virtues of numbers and order. To get her off my back, I agreed to be tutored by the tutor of her choice, promising to do my best, to get past my number 4 problem, or as she called it: "my problem number four."

My tutor was the arithmetic star of the class. Since the only time he could tutor me was late in the evening, his bed and mine were moved after dinner into the dining room. As soon as the lights were turned off and everyone was getting ready to take off for the night, Yuval began drilling me with the numbers.

After much going around in a circle, we started talking about it; "What if we did not call number four number four?" he asked.

"What will we call it?" I asked. "Number five?" He didn't laugh; I did.

"How about if we just think about number four as something other than number four?"

"Like what?" I said. He got me going.

"How about an upside-down chair?" he said.

I thought it a brilliant idea. But when I tried to picture it to myself, I got confused again. "Does it mean that twenty plus one upside-down chair, divided by one upside-down chair, is one upside-down chair?" I asked.

"You are on the way!" he said, laughing. I wasn't. But I did feel lighter when I fell asleep that night.

I was cold that night, dogs were barking in my dreams, and upside-down chairs and swastikas were everywhere. When he woke me up in the morning, I was sleeping on the bare springs of the bed, using the mattress as a cover. (I had done it while asleep, without getting out of bed). My classmates, waiting for breakfast, were standing around my bed, staring at me, shaking their heads left and right, over and over, giggling.

Carrying all those upside-down chairs in my head, instead of a simple number4, I realized much later, was just a symptom of other problems. I had a problem expressing myself in clear, understandable everyday terms. I still do. Which, of course, I realized (when it was too late) was all part of the same upside-down chair business.*

With a few variations, that is how I have lived the first fifty years. I am now working to see what, if anything, I should change for the next ten broken chairs plus ten years.

*   *   *

It soon became obvious that everyone around me disliked chaos as much as I disliked rules, so with number four still hanging over my head, sinking deeper into trouble was inevitable. It was next to impossible to teach me anything. It still is. I was equally bad in all subjects—except, of course, math, in which I continued to be a disaster. What made matters worse was homework, which for reasons still not entirely clear, I did not do. It wasn't that I had anything against homework, per se. But since without doing homework, I still wasn't the worst pupil in the class, I remember thinking, "Why should I do homework?" To make sure no teacher could say, "He did *my* homework," which would have gotten me in real trouble, I thought it best to treat all subjects and teachers equally. But I miscalculated; I did a lot of that then.

It was a bright morning when our teacher quietly cornered me with a chilly smile. "You won't get anywhere in this place if you won't do your homework," she said. I was very surprised to hear her say that, since from the very first day, Peter and I were the only ones trying to go somewhere. Anywhere! And every time we did, they sent the soldiers after us. Afterward, Peter would get beaten so badly that he had to rest for many days before he was ready to try again.

But of course, I misunderstood her. What she meant was "somewhere," as in a future. My future. Understanding what people meant was just one of my many problems then. It still is. I stared at her blankly. "But everyone thinks about the future," she said, as though it was the most self-evident, natural thing in the world.

"Back where I came from," I tried to explain, "the one thing I never did—in fact, no one I knew did—was think about the future. It wasn't practical. It simplified life to pretend that there was no future. "Tomorrow," I said, "is the furthest I ever thought of."

---

* Peter told Beverly that it was not until years later that he realized that the number 4 must have reminded him of a swastika.

While she was looking at me blankly, I quickly added that I had no home. Which, of course, was the wrong thing to say, but the cold wet silence hanging between us was scary. I had to say something, and that was the only thing circling in my mind at the time. "What do you mean," she said, sitting back. "Didn't I tell you on the first day that my home is your home?" She did. But as I told you, that day had turned out badly. In fact, it was one of the days I tried not to think about. And every time I did, it drove me to run away again.

Of course, I could have told her that every time she was beating Peter I felt like she was beating me too. But saying that, I was sure, would have gotten me in more trouble than I already was in. Being the coward, I took to drifting away from her shining black eyes staring at me from an unsmiling mask of the future.

What I did finally say to her was something to the effect that everything here seemed very different from what they said to me in Marseille, when I asked about Palestine. It was a stupid thing to say. I could hardly believe my ears, but I had an irresistible urge to let her know! "What did they say?" she asked. Against my better judgment, I proceeded to tell her: "In Palestine, I will be free! Never have to fear or worry about a thing; it is our paradise."

"So?" she asked.

"It's not like that at all," I said. "This could not possibly be the place where only the most lucky of people get to go to."

"What do you mean?" she asked, sitting straight up, as if bitten. I was free-falling now; it wasn't like I could turn back. So I went on, falling, telling her that if the somewhere she is talking about is anything like this place, I could not see the point of wanting to go anywhere! There was a bad, long silence. She was looking past me into space. Thinking she probably did not understand me, I went on, making it worse, blabbering about how the place reminds me of the camp and all that I remember from over there.

Even then I knew I was losing it, just as Peter did the first day in the mini-animal farm. I was bent on kicking her and the place in the balls; no one could have stopped me. Like you say, "I had had it." I did not often, but when I did, I did.

"You are always alone," she said a day later. "You should play with the others."

"I don't like to play," I said.

"But everyone likes to play. You will not feel alone if you do," she said, leaning forward, trying to peek into my eyes, smiling that same cold smile again.

It was then that I first noticed that she had something against the idea of being alone, disliked it, probably as much as I disliked the idea of being together. "It's the together thing that I can't stand. Everything together: get up, wash, eat, play, sleep all together all day long, every day—it drives us crazy! The one thing I want most of all," I tried to explain, "is to be alone. I cannot see anyone wanting to live like this."

Two cold naked eyes were looking at me from an unsmiling mask. My efforts to explain myself further were futile, she was elsewhere, gone, her black eyes were fixed at a point far away beyond the horizon. *Now I have gotten myself in real trouble,* I thought, *the kind I may not be able to drift away from.*

Wanting to be alone was considered antisocial, scary enough to deserve being sent to a doctor, a head doctor, a shrink. He had a proper beard and asked a lot of questions. The only one I remember to this day is the one about the train. "The train is coming, you know that something on the track is wrong, the train will derail. What are you going to do?"

"I will run away as fast as I can," I said. "And then?" he asked.

"Then nothing." I said. *I never did find out what he told the kibbutz afterward, but they left me alone, for a while.*

SHEEP

Kibbutz Afek, 1950

"The sheep that are due soon have blue markings and the ones with red marks are recovering from injury, so watch out for them," Ludvik said on my first day before I was to take the sheep out to graze in the hills. "The donkey," he said, "will refuse to go out of the shade. You are on your own there. But when the sun goes down and you begin to head homeward, he will start running. You must hold him back, don't let him run, or the sheep will follow and they will lose all their milk." Bending down, holding me by the shirt, looking straight into my eyes, making sure I understood him, he continued. "And there are the fields of melons, squash, and cucumbers on the way, which belong to the Arabs. The sheep can't resist. You must anticipate them. Once they're in, it's too late!" His still pointing finger hooked on the top button of my shirt. "The Arabs will be coming down here giving me hell, and I will be coming after you!"

From then on, every afternoon before taking them out, Ludvick drew me a map of the path to the grazing grounds. And every time the sheep did break through to the Arabs' fields, there was Ludvick, at the end of his stick, thundering all over the kibbutz, looking for me.

*   *   *

She redoubled her effort, setting on Peter at the slightest provocation, or for no reason at all. For his part, he continued to resist her the only way he could; taking her beatings in silence, refusing to acknowledge her. It was as if the two of them were caught in a struggle to the end. She, all-powerful, set on breaking him, no matter what. He, unbearably frail, defenseless, but with a spirit that wouldn't break. It never occurred to her that she might not succeed, no matter how much heart she put in to it.

"The one thing you shouldn't do," I kept telling him, "is draw attention to yourself. Your clowning is getting you in trouble." I was a coward. My way out was to retreat, making myself as small a target as possible. He'd look at me for a long time and say nothing.

I did not understand then that perhaps he had retreated as far as he could; he was at the end, with nowhere to go, nothing left to do, but to go on doing what he was doing. Doing his act was his way of declaring that he was alive! His way of hanging on to himself.

New York, 1970s

Joe: Now why would a woman who had recognition, connections, influence, and power—everything a member can ever hope to have—set on breaking someone like Peter?

Peter: As I began writing this account, I had few doubts about it. But today, I see that she played a minor role in this story. I suspect that we'd all like to pose the question as you pose it. Largely because it diverts our attention from ourselves, the nature of the kibbutz, and the role of the nationalist doctrine in this story.

J: How do you figure that?

P: By dancing his unbearable weakness, he turned his misfortune into a spectacle, a joke. He was mocking himself, but he was mocking her too, in front of her children. With his ghastly dance of the meek on the side of the road, he was stalking the "grand march" itself, stealing the show. And that is what Esther Katzenelson couldn't take, nor could the kibbutz. It was the end. Great movements that set out to change the world do not take kindly to being laughed at, much less by a pathetic weakling like Peter. His laughter was the kind that raises eyebrows, questions, perhaps even doubts about the "grand march" itself and its cherished myth about the Jews of Europe—those Jews who were afflicted by fear, endemic fear, that like a moth ate away at what they were, reducing them to living on their knees and finally walking into the ovens, leaving them feeling guilty, impotent, eternally resentful. They represented everything that the Zionist establishment was desperate to turn its back on and felt contempt for. The "children of the dream" were not supposed to be infected with the past. That's why they were separated from their parents. Peter was not in the cards. And when he tumbled out of the closet, she lost it. He was supposed to be like me: hide, lick his wounds out of sight at night under the sheets. But he wouldn't. He refused to play by the rules, was blatant about it. The notion that his misfortune was his own fault seemed to have completely escaped him.

J: Do you think she was evil?

P: I do not. The evils of this century, I believe, are a product of a social climate rather then the work of a few evil men. Our teacher was as much a victim of a bleak, hard, pessimistic view of life, a political philosophy, which the late Israeli historian Jacob Talmon approvingly described as a "divine and creative madness, which not only stills all fear and hesitation but also makes for clarity of vision in a landscape bathed in a lurid, distorting light."

J: I see your point. But it is difficult to feel sympathy for her or sense the tragedy you are talking about.

P: I believe she resigned herself and had no consciousness of herself or her actions. Her situation was dictated by the principle concerns of the collective. Her tragedy is that, although unaware, she was diminished by this "divine madness" as we all are.

J: Do you think the kibbutz members were indifferent to you?

P: I have no way of knowing how they felt. What I do know is that there were members, who at first seeing Peter black and blue, were moved by compassion to stand up for him but didn't, were embarrassed seeing him black and blue a second time. The more she beat him, the worse they felt. It was then just a question of time, before they found themselves in the corner with his teacher, rooting for his expulsion. But I do not think they were indifferent to Peter. Given the system they had created, they had little if any choice.

J: What you are suggesting is that it was Peter's very tenacity to hold
       on, refusing to disappear, that made him increasingly more visible,
       eventually forcing the kibbutz to expel him.
P: It was.
J: It sounds terrible.
P: Terrible for whom?
J: For everyone.
P: The height of irony.
J: What do you mean?
P: I mean that the "divine madness" created a generation of Israelis, fearful,
       armed to the teeth with nuclear weapons, as obsessed by insecurity as
       the European Diaspora ever was.

DAVID K.

Kibbutz Afek, 1950s

While most everyone else was writing editorials about Generalisimo
Francisco Franco and Hitler, David K. took their threats so seriously that he
volunteered to fight them. The possibility that one day his deed would be held
against him, he said, seemed preposterous. But he underestimated history and
overestimated man's capacity to forget. America was looking for enemies, and
K. was just what the moment called for. So K. closed his plumbing business
in Brooklyn, packed up his life, and set out for the Promised Land, arriving
at the kibbutz, no longer by the sea,* with his wife, five daughters, and the
one on the way.

The only American in a kibbutz made up of Jews from Russia and
Poland, he became an instant curiosity, if not a celebrity. He did wonders for
our plumbing, his wife washed dishes in the collective kitchen, and their five
daughters added a new bit of "hope you're free" glow to the lives of the children.

Later, counting the kibbutz votes after the national elections, one vote
was found to have been cast for the Communist Party. It wasn't illegal, the
party was on the ballot, but voting for it apparently was another thing, a
sin, unpardonable. K. was one of two suspects. Next to nothing was known
about the other suspect: Ernst, an eccentric middle-aged Englishman, with

---

* A few years after Peter arrived, his kibbutz moved further inland and changed
  its name from Mishmar Haryam to Afek.

a body of an Arabian racehorse, who was into yoga, meditation, and other exotic stuff to maintain his perfect body, all which was beyond the interests of kibbutzniks at the time. "When consideration of your membership in the kibbutz comes up, it will be turned down," K. was told. "You may stay while you are looking for other arrangements."

The irony of having volunteered to fight Fascism in Spain, thereby becoming an enemy of Zionism, took K. by surprise. "What I can't understand," he said over and over, shaking his head, "is that for years, they took my money, they came after me, badgered me. You never know, one day you may not feel that safe in Brooklyn—where would you go then? So I come, and what do you know? I am an enemy of Zionism! they tell me and throw me out. I can't understand it. What does that make of Zionism? You tell me?"

Three people were expelled from the kibbutz in my years there: Peter, because he didn't fit in; an electrician who stole equipment; and K. who was suspected to have cast the offending vote. Like Peter, K. had no say in the matter. His fate was decided by a show of hands of those present at a Saturday night general meeting. A simple majority did it. He neither asked for, nor was offered, a fair hearing.

CHICKENS

Kibbutz Afek, 1952

It was around that time that I began to steal chickens. At the beginning, it had something to do with our "hanging out." On the side of the barbed wire in the field, around a fire singing sentimental Russian songs, late into the night, someone (it was probably a girl) mentioned she would have liked to have something to eat. I was working at the chicken house at the time and without really thinking about it asked, "How about a chicken?" "A chicken?" she said in a way that was clear "chicken" was the last thing on her mind. But others picked up on it.

One normally had chicken on Passover or when one was sick. And then it was boiled to death, that is to say, it was boiled to make soup until there was no more chicken left on the chicken. Here was our chance to have the real thing. Sex was definitely frowned on, so chicken it was.

It was easy the first time, I knew where the key was. Once inside the chicken house, the light from the moon was enough to get me to where the chickens were sitting next to each other, in a perfect row on a kind of broomstick hanging by a wire from the ceiling, asleep. The trick was to get the chicken quietly in the sack without waking the others. It went without a hitch, but I was nervous on my way back with two chickens in the sack. While I was fetching the chickens (I say "fetched" because we reasoned that since everything in the kibbutz belonged to everyone, it couldn't really be called stealing), others improvised a pot, spoons, knives, and plates, and we had our chickens eaten well before sunrise.

NEW SHOES

We were in for new shoes, all twenty-four of us. We climbed on the back of the truck and were on our way, singing revolutionary Russian songs all the way to Haifa. It seems that way back before I even knew the value of money; I had an expensive taste, which did not make this undertaking any easier. But it was an important revelation and a lesson I never forgot.

The store was in an alley with a door in the port district. The shoes were standing alone in a row, shoulder to shoulder, on glass shelves in the window. Glued to the inside heel of each odd shoe was a piece of paper with a number. The other shoe was packed in one of the many shoe boxes going up all the way to the ceiling.

There were no prices, of course. So on spotting a shoe one liked, one had to run to the metapelet, pull at her apron until she turned, and wrote the number on her piece of paper next to one's name. She would then turn and read the numbers to a man running up and down a tall ladder, pulling and replacing shoe boxes in a cloud of dust as fast as he could. When he found the right box, he'd throw it down to the waiting hands of a bright-eyed assistant in a smock, appropriately gray. On landing, each box produced its own burst of dust. The bright-eyed assistant opened the box and, with a dusty smile, handed the shoes to the metapelet, who in turn called the kid who had asked for that pair. After taking his place in a line, he would wait until one of the two chairs in the shop was available so he could take his shoes off, put on the new pair, and look at his shoes in the small mirror. No one was in a hurry. If the shoes fit, the metapelet would hand the shoes back to the assistant who would put the shoes back in the box, write the price and the name of the kid on a piece of paper, hand it to the metapelet who would take it to the cash register where the wife of the man on the ladder, who conducted this operation with a soprano pitch and a quick hand, made out a bill that the metapelet signed, and handed the box back with the shoes to the metapelet who in turn would call out for the proper kid and hand him his shoes. And so it went.

"These are too expensive," she said. Of course, I was surprised, I must have been elsewhere when she talked about price. It was probably my sulking that moved the bright-eyed assistant to suggest, "Let him try them on." Standing in my new shoes, I was Gene Kelly for the moment. Did she know of Gene Kelly? We saw the same movies every Tuesday. She must have. "Not too sturdy," she said, shaking her head at my shoes. "Will fall apart in the first rain," she said as she handed them back to the assistant, obviously unimpressed by Gene Kelly. "Better look for another pair," she said. Somehow the idea of giving up on Gene Kelly for a pair of sturdy shoes that would last a lifetime in the mud seemed absurd: I am not going to look for another pair, no matter what she or anyone else said or did, I decided. By now everyone was done, ready to go. Her white apron was gray. "Pick up a pair," she said patiently, "any pair." She was a saint!

"But I don't like any of them."

"It's just a pair of shoes!" she said, pleading for common sense.

But the connection between Gene Kelly and common sense eluded me completely. If I couldn't have the shoes I liked, I saw no point in having shoes at all, and I remained silent, sulking.

"But what will you do without shoes?" she asked.

"I will manage," I said.

"But you must have shoes, the winter is coming," she said with true concern. Which gave me the idea that I should definitely hold out, refuse all shoes, no matter what. I climbed on the truck and we were off, back to the kibbutz. Singing Russian revolutionary songs all the way.

No one paid much attention when, a few weeks later, it began to drizzle, but it soon began raining buckets. Sitting on a bench across from me, the metapelet leaned over. "So you see! Now what will you do?" As she said it, I saw myself entering the public dining room barefoot. And there, in a flash, I realized what was my next move for the Gene Kelly shoes. I remained silent. Of course, I was not going to tell her.

Even with a little rain, the kibbutz, moved inland and no longer by the sea, was mostly mud. Sidewalks connecting the houses were far off in the future. In the meantime, everyone was shlepping in the mud. As I expected, walking barefoot into the dining hall, mud up to my knees, was a big success: "Where are your shoes?" "What do you mean, you don't have any?" And so the next day I was given money to go back to Haifa on the bus to fetch my "Gene Kelly" shoes. It was by those shoes that I was eventually transported out, away from the Kibbutz by the Sea.

CHAPTER 2

THE CHILDREN OF THE DREAM

I was awed by my classmates. Everything seemed easy for them, they were uncomplicated, straightforward. They were strong, healthy, sure of themselves. They seemed to fear nothing. I realize how socially awkward I was, and I knew in my gut that I would never be like them.

I was a fearful, calculating weakling. I was tentative about every move, walking on eggs. I was afraid of the dark, of the noises coming from my mattress, of my dreams. To this day, I avoid opening the mail or answering the door. I panic before every photo assignment, thinking disaster lurks just around the corner.

My classmates were what Bruno Bettelheim called *The Children of the Dream,* the apple of the kibbutz eye, the future. *The Children of the Dream* were not going to be like their parents. The accordion, Russian revolutionary songs, Slavic soulful sentimental tunes replaced the sound of the fiddle, the clarinet. The sound of Jewish mamas singing old heart-rending lullabies was out, a part of the past, as was Mark Chagall's lovers in the sky and cows flying over the moon. The "new Jew," they hoped, was going to be selfless, without angst, strong, fearless, without cultural hang-ups or guilt.

It must have been clear to anyone looking at us that Peter and I did not and most likely never would fit in. We were the past the kibbutz was trying to get rid of, Peter and I, two nightmares among the children of the dream. We belonged to a very different fairy tale.

Forgetting—organized forgetting—was what the kibbutz was largely about. Yesterday's actions were obscured by today's actions; and the strongest link binding us to a life, constantly eaten away by forgetting, was nostalgia. Remorseful nostalgia and remorseless skepticism were the two ends of the scale that animated life on the boat that was the kibbutz. Years later, watching the news from Israel I knew that sooner or later I would see these same children of the dream doing their duty in the ghettos of the West bank and Gaza. Thirty years later, David Grossman in *The Yellow Wind* tells of kibbutzim-expelling members who refused to serve in Lebanon or take part in enforcing the "iron fist." *There, but for the grace of Providence, go I*, I thought when I read it.

For much of the sixties, Bruno Bettelheim, the noted child psychologist, was a cult figure within the East Coast liberal establishment. His New York lecture on *The Children of the Dream* was sold out. My wife, Luba, who had her own reservations about Bettleheims's theories of child rearing, was as eagerly looking forward to hearing him as I was, hoping, of course, to be vindicated.

He stood in a spot of light, on a darkened stage, commenting on silent film footage of kibbutz toddlers by themselves, at play, with peers, with parents, and grandparents. Throughout his running commentary, he kept at his thesis: "Parents and grandparents spoil their children." When the scene shifted to inside a kibbutz home where a doting grandmother reached out to embrace a baby, Bettleheim declared that grandparents weren't just spoiling the little ones, they were in fact an impediment to their social development and adjustment to communal living, kibbutz life. "Letting them grow in the environment of their peers, with minimum contact with parents and grandparents," he argued, "is the key to producing the children of the dream." Judging from the mutterings in the audience, it was clear that his views were not to the liking of this crowd, and he sensed it.

For some time after his presentation was finished, it was uncertain whether or not he would stay for a discussion period. A room was finally made available upstairs. Within minutes, it was packed with apprehensive parents and seething grandmothers, waiting for their turn. He sat alone, regally, in the right corner of a new leather sofa, with the air of old imperial Vienna about him. The bright light of conviction was shining in his eyes. He responded to all questions in a dismissive, contemptuous tone.

"Did you notice anything strange about him?" Luba, asked on our way home. "I think he was out to scandalize," I said. "And much of what he said was said to idealize the lives of children left at the mercy of their peers, metapelets, and teachers—many unqualified and all unsupervised. But other than that, I didn't see anything strange about him."

"Didn't you notice him stabbing the sofa with the tip of his ballpoint pen, as if to drive every word he spoke into the minds of his audience?"

"I did!"

'Something was scary about this man," she said as we walked home. She has some of the sharpest eyes I have ever come across. Ten years later, some of the children under his care came out with accounts that he was tyrannical, violent, and that he had physically abused them.

THE NEW TEACHER

Kibbutz Afek, 1950

She was a voluptuous blond, a "Turkish delight," pink all over, almost as wide as she was tall. "I am your new Bible teacher," she said in a firm, no-nonsense tone. We had never had a Bible lesson. "We are going to start by reading from Solomon's 'Song of Songs,'" she announced, her beady pink eyes sweeping the room in a slow pan, from left to right, taking us in, one by one. "But before we start, I want everyone to tell me their name, the name of their parents, and what they do." I could hear a voice urging me to leave the class, but I stayed glued to my chair, unable to move.

Some weeks earlier, I had received the second letter from my grandmother in Australia. In addition to asking me what I wanted for my thirteenth birthday, she told me that late in 1944 she had received a note from the Gestapo notifying her that her daughter died in Ravensbrucke. It confirmed what I feared all along: my mother was dead. Zeve[8] read it sitting on the porch, translating Grandmother's letter into Hebrew, reading without stopping, his words receding into a milky foglike cloud of nothingness.

Germany, 1944

She dressed me in short lederhosen that morning. We left the house in the dark, quietly. Once out of town, Mother started running; I trailed behind, holding on to her hand. At first, we ran on dirt roads, narrow trails, past waking roosters and barking dogs. The grass was tall and damp; there was much poison ivy. As the sun rose in the sky, we went into the tall wheat. I remember her hand gripping my hand. In a blur, the back of her feet raced ahead. I could not keep up and kept stumbling. We stopped for a while and then went on running in a sea of wheat. At the end of the day, a farmer took us in. "He has strong legs," I remember him saying, standing at the door of his barn, looking us over. He brought us food and water and woke us up before dawn.

We went on, running all day, as we had the day before. It was late when we arrived, Leipzig was dark and empty. Within minutes of entering the apartment, there were knocks on the door. It was the Gestapo, demanding to see our papers. One of them lifted me up from behind, dragging me into a corner. Another started pulling at my pants. I knew what he was after and tried to fend him off, kicking my feet in the air, trying to hold on to my pants, but he managed to pull them down. It was all the identification they needed. They took us to the police station.

They came for my mother in the morning. As they took her away, out of the cell, one of the Gestapo men turned his head, facing me; he said, "You will see your mother soon," and closed the door.

Kibbutz Afek, c. 1950

At first, after I got the letter from my grandmother, I pretended that nothing had happened. But the lump was growing in the pit of my stomach. Before, I used to hold wagers in my head: if I succeeded in winning a race, skipping over a stretch of sidewalk without landing on the dividing lines, flipping coins, betting on whether it would rain or be sunny the next day. Winning meant she is alive; she will find me one day. When I lost, I just repeated the wager until I won.

I slept nights in the 4' x 5' room Zeve* shared with his wife while the new children's house was being built. He was a kind man, constantly talking about not having time to write. I started wetting my bed, spending the better part of most nights lying awake, trying to figure out a way to dry off my sheets, while he and his wife slept.

I couldn't eat. The lump in my stomach was with me all day long. So was the smell of death. "Something has died in the forest," they said. After finding a place to throw up, I would feel relief, for a while. I wanted to hide, fold, give up. But in the kibbutz one is just a part of the whole, one belongs to the whole, one must forever participate: eat, sleep, play, do as others do, when they do it. The mere thought of wanting to be alone was an unkosher thought, subversive.

At night, I curled up under my sheet and cried, pretending I was asleep. One day, a thought flashed through my mind: it could be a mistake, even the Gestapo could make a mistake, and so I went on, holding on.

But now, the Bible teacher was coming at me with the deliberate pace of a steamroller, as one child after another recited the names of their mother and father. I felt the ground begin to give way. I sat there, paralyzed by a sense of inevitable doom. There was a silence, it stretched out. A miracle is taking place, I thought. She has given up, is going away, onto the next kid. I looked at her. She was reclining in her chair, her head tilted back, eyes closed.

---

* Zeve was a German-speaking kibbutz member who befriended Peter.

A limp hand was reaching slowly into her cleavage; when it came up to the light, her fingers were moist with perspiration. She opened her eyes, looked closely at her fingers, rubbing them against each other, feeling the texture of her sweat. Then, closing her eyes, she brought them up to her nose, sniffed them, sucking the air deep into her lungs, holding her breath for an instant, savoring the aroma. Then she let the air out, slowly, with a long quiet sigh of satisfaction. When she opened her eyes, they were fixed on me. Little pale pink eyes with a reddish tint, her eyebrows blended into the pale pink of her face. "I have all the time in the world," she said. Having made her point, she closed her eyes and sent her hand back in to her cleavage.

She is as determined to wait me out as I am to hold on to my secret, I thought. By now there was a pool of tears in the back of my eyeballs. I was fighting a losing battle to hold them back, hoping someone in my class would say something, anything that might stop her. I looked around me. My classmates were looking past me, as if they had never seen me before. I was a stranger. The dam gave way, my sorrows came rushing at me, a stream of warm salty tears came flooding down my face. I crumbled into a wet mass of hiccups, gasping for breath, sobbing in my chair, telling her the best I could that my mother and father were dead. Without responding, she went to the next kid and on to the next and then on to Solomon's Song of Songs.

For some days, I walked around the place dazed. I talked to no one; my classmates went on as though it had never happened: it could have been worse, but it was all part of the world that had followed me from "over there," best forgotten.

I was walking out of the shower, in a cloud of steam. Silhouettes were standing, others sitting on wooden benches talking in the steam. Full-length mirrors were hanging from the walls. Drying myself, I looked in the mirror. It was steamed up, I couldn't see myself. I wiped the steam off with my hand. The face staring at me wasn't mine, it was smiling. I went to the next panel, wiped off the steam, the face streaked with water looking back at me was the same face. I went to the next panel, and the next, and the next . . . The same smiling face was looking back at me.

I ran out naked into the rain with my rubber boots on. I kept running until one of my boots got stuck in the mud. In trying to dislodge it, the other boot got stuck too. I left the boots behind and kept running. Exhausted, I stopped. I was knee-deep, sinking in mud, getting deeper. People naked, wet with rain, came out of the fog, walking by like sleepwalkers, disappearing in the fog. Others were sitting naked, stooped in wooden chairs with straight backs. Ahead, sticking out of the fog line was the roof of a railroad car. As I came close, I saw it was empty, it had no wheels, there were no tracks. I climbed on and sat down on a wooden bench. When I opened my eyes, the train was moving.

Kibbutz Afek, 1954

"You have a bad reputation," said Talma many years later, on our second date. When I asked her what she meant, she said, "You had a temper tantrum when the Bible teacher arrived. You climbed on a table and pissed into the middle of the classroom." Astonished, I asked her, "Where did you get this story?" "From my mother," she said.

Talma's account of the incident stunned me. I suppose because I thought that everyone wanted to forget the incident as much as I did. The notion of the incident floating around as part of the local gossip was chilling, sinking in slowly, entering from the top of my head like a beam of ice boring slowly down my spine. Sitting under a tree, I sank into a silence of shame, fear, anger, and a feeling of futility. "What's wrong?" Talma kept asking. I could not bring myself to say anything. How am I going to tell her what really happened that morning in the Bible class? I thought. And then I realized. It was not a question of whether she believed my version of the incident or her mother's; the story would always be out there, in the air we breathe. There was nothing I or anyone else could do about it. I was beaten down, too despondent to find the words to describe how I felt or to recount the story. It was useless to say anything.

Thirty years later, sitting in Shakespeare's Restaurant in Greenwich Village, out of nowhere, the words, feelings, and tears all came together. I recounted the scene as it happened to my therapy group of eight dear men and women who, for ten years, had been with me every Tuesday on a journey of self-rediscovery. I crumpled as I did then, onto my hamburger and chips, unable to stop.

CHAPTER 3

IN THE LAND WITH NO MEMORY

THE AUDITION

Israel, 1961

"You are the most normal person I know," Anna Sokolow said at a party in Haifa. I was taken aback, surprised, but I was also flattered. I had grafted a new me on the old one; like a pianist that has gone deaf and lost the sense of touch, I remembered the keys. It was working.

"Rooms" is dance as theater, theater as dance, pure Anna Sokolow. The title of the solo part I was to dance was "Panic." I am reclining on the back of a chair, asleep, the stage is dark and quiet. A spotlight hits my face. I wake up in a panic. It was an exhausting piece. After weeks of rehearsals, I could barely do it every Tuesday without collapsing before the end.

"That's not it," she'd say, shaking her head from side to side. "The spirit isn't there. Imagine you are alone in a small room in a big city like New York" was the way she set it up for me. "It is summer, you live in this tiny little room in a big city like New York. You wake up from a nightmare drenched in sweat, trying to break out, but you can't! Your dream is closing in on you . . . Go. Go on, show me," she'd say, waving a graceful frail hand, bent ever so slightly from the wrist in front of her face, pushing the air aside as if it was water around her, turning on one heel, and slowly walking away like a matador from the bull.

"That's not it," she would say, her head turning away, her right arm rising in an "I give up" motion, all over again. "You are holding back!" I did not understand. We fought about it for weeks. She was tough. I was falling off my feet feeling bewildered, depressed. As opening night loomed, that chair on the stage was with me wherever I went. It was all I thought about, but it did no good. "That's not it," she would say, over and over. I began thinking of leaving the company.

It was on the morning of opening night that I remembered the kibbutz. It was the memory of my first day, curled up like a black bug, trapped under the sheet, that I took with me to opening night. Anna was beaming. "You were as good as the original," she said as she hugged me. I was flying in heaven. The original was Alvin Ailey.

Did I dance that well? Or did she see in me a world going deaf, losing the sense of touch and was in her way, ringing the bell.

I must have played well though, because it was this piece that I danced for José Limon, Anthony Tudor, Paul Draper, and Alfredo Corvino at the Juilliard auditions. There was a total silence when I was done.

Some months later Martha Graham, looking for a dancer, called Anthony Tudor, in whose classes I never managed to keep my footing. To my great surprise, I learned later that it was he who recommended me.

MY AMERICAN RELATIVES

New York, 1963

I called them as soon as I felt settled in New York. The first family were tailors with a dry-cleaning store on the Upper West Side. The other family was in noodles. I had just been accepted by the Juilliard School of Music as a full scholarship student in the dance department. They invited me to dinner, and on the appointed day, I took the subway to the Upper West Side to meet relatives I did not know I had until a few months earlier. HJ, my lawyer in Berlin, knowing of my plans to go to New York, sort of let it slip out. "Do you know that you have relatives in New York?" I was as hard a nut then as I ever was. Nothing in me moved. He handed me a piece of paper with their names and addresses, and that was that. The hard part was calling them. Once I did, I did not think about it until I was on the subway, looking at the note HJ had given me in Berlin. I remember briefly wondering, why did they invite me? But I quickly put it out of out of mind.

The tailors, in their '60s, lived in a modest Upper West Side apartment where one enters directly into the living room. I was drawn to a photograph of a woman, sitting at a piano, when I heard a voice behind me say, "Do you know who that is?" When I did not answer, the voice continued, "It is your mother, would you like to have it?" I just stood there, frozen, staring at it. I realized that I had forgotten what my mother looked like. Tears were lurking behind the sockets of my eyes, but I was not about to let them see me cry. I did not turn for a while. When I did, they were sitting on a couch. It was the man who broke the silence saying, "We want you to know that we did everything we could to save you and your mother." I felt as if I was hit by a one knockout punch, leaving me out cold on my feet, staring into space.

The spell was broken by the arrival of the other family. The "noodle man" was a short, heavy-set, jovial, cigar-smoking man. He came in like a big wind, sweeping everyone off their seats and into his long, blue Cadillac. He drove it hard, deep into Queens, the cigar stuck in his mouth, leading the way. He did not take it out until we got there. Much of what he said escaped me, but I understood that he was talking about his pride and joy—the house. When he finally slowed down, he pointed it out. It was a minor Tudor castle with a Queens twist.

It was not possible to miss the fact that they had made it. They had two cars, each with its own garage and remote control operated doors, which he proudly demonstrated. They had countless bedrooms and bathrooms. There was a television in the kitchen, dining room, living room, and every bedroom, all operated by remote control. Some he demonstrated. When we came to the master bedroom he said, "Just look at this." He lay down on his back, and pushed a button. The bed started to vibrate under him. He had not taken his cigar out of his mouth since the West Side. Now, tiny rings of smoke rose from his cigar, giving him a look of a locomotive held up by an invisible force, shaking in place.

"It helps me fall asleep," he said. I watched the smoke rise from his shaking body, forming little rings, when a voice came over an intercom, "We will be eating in a few minutes." He pushed the button, and for a moment his body was absolutely still and silent. Then, without turning his head he asked, "Did you ever have a roast beef dinner?" I said I had not. "Well," he said, "you are going to have one tonight. The best! There is nothing like a roast beef dinner, you'll see." He took the cigar out of his mouth, turned, got up and led the way downstairs. When we were all seated his wife asked me, "How was your trip?" as though I had just come from Pittsburgh. I said it was fine. The conversation seemed to have sunk, right there. We were like five matzoh balls made of stone, drowned in a bowl of golden chicken soup.

Her husband, having put away his cigar, looked more like an elephant without his trunk than the successful "Goodman's noodle man." He turned to me, eyebrows slightly raised, asking, "How's the roast beef?' It was bleeding, but I said it was very good. He then said something about installing new doors on the closets of the house, so they could be opened and closed electronically. And gave the latest news from the noodle front. My mind kept drifting from my plate back to the tailor's house where my mother was sitting at the piano in the picture on the wall.

At the end of the evening, they drove me back to my apartment in Hell's Kitchen, on Forty-ninth and Ninth. I thanked them for the dinner and invited them to a dance concert at Juilliard at which I was going to perform. I sent them tickets but they did not show up. In fact, I never heard from them again. For a while, I wondered why. Was it something I said? Or did not say? Why did they invite me in the first place? Eventually, I forgot about them and went on with my life. It was not until many years later when the *New York Times* carried an article about the disbanding of the ill-fated Goldberg Commission that I got the first whiff that during the nineteen forties, America's Jews did not do what they now wished they had done. Looking back on that dinner now, I wonder whether there was really much we could talk about. It seems that all they had to say to me was said by the tailors. By declining their offer of the picture of my mother, I instinctively held on to the halo of my misfortune, and their feet were chained to what they felt they should have done but didn't. Did they hear a new skeleton in their closets?

New York, 1988

I made a copy of the Yellow Star and joined some fifty protesters, mostly Palestinians wrapped up in their keffiyehs, at the Israeli Consulate to protest against the "iron fist." The police were out on foot, on horseback, in patrol cars and vans, at all four corners of the block, just in case. It was one of those nasty November days, when only New York's homeless were on the streets.

Some distance ahead, an old couple was shuffling in the circle of protestors, behind the steam of their breath. They seemed frail and wooden in a circle overwhelmingly young. His arm was wrapped around her, protecting her from the cold. She kept wiping her face with a mittened hand. I thought I saw tears in her eyes. When I saw them next, she was no longer wiping her face, her tears were flowing freely. "She can't take it," he said, talking to himself. I wanted to say something to comfort him but could find no words. We shuffled along side by side. Calls for justice and a free Palestine, coming from an electronic tin WM, were drowned by the WMs of midtown traffic honking the lunch hour away.

I turned at a tug at my sleeve. He was still shaking his head, "I . . . can't . . . can't understand it . . . ," he repeated, over and over, shaking his head, his breath dissolving in the harsh winter light, "I can't understand it . . . I just can't . . . understand! I was with the Brigade in Spain . . . with my brother . . .

he died there . . . my wife survived Ravensbrucke . . . and now . . . this! I can't understand . . . ! She's been up . . . crying for days . . . We will be dying as Fascists, in a Jewish city."

*   *   *

JOE

Joe, my analyst, was looking out his window with its view of the World Trade Center, shaking his head at my taking part in the demonstration. It upsets him. He is as far from the Jewish far right as North is from South. In fact, politically we agree on practically everything, except on the issue of Israel. Where instinct takes over, complex issues are reduced to "us against them, you against me" old-fashioned loyalty. "It's an act of self-hate," he said, shaking his head at the window.

"In other words, you are saying that if I am not with you, I am against you, against your ancestors, as well as my own ancestors. I am against myself—an anti-Semite?" "It's an act of self-hate," he repeated, shaking his head, looking out at the horizon. As I walked away, his words echoed through me all the way down Ninth Street and on to next Tuesday.

Over the weekend, a conference on liberalism in America sponsored by *Tikkun* magazine was held in New York's Madison Square Garden. At the morning's opening session, Edward Said suggested that the process of reconciliation between Jews and Palestinians would depend, in part, on whether Jews are prepared to bear witness to what they have done to Palestinians. There followed a long silence; no one from the panel or the audience responded to Mr. Said's words.

In the afternoon, a young man from Seattle stood up and said, "I am active in Hillel and in my congregation's many activities. I know about the Holocaust. I know all about Israel, I am committed to it, but I don't really know what it means to be Jewish." He was followed by others expressing similar sentiments, but no one from the panel or the audience responded to the dilemma raised by the young man from Seattle.

Incredulous at the statement, I asked around, "Did he mean what I thought he meant?" "Yes," I was told, "in America Jews believe in the Holocaust and worship Israel." I was amazed. I had been living in New York for more than twenty-five years then and always thought of it as "a Jewish city." In a way, I was like the old man, shaking his head in the night. I have always considered myself Jewish, but to worship a state? It was a revelation:

"Could that be what Joe was talking about?" Judy Chicago's memorial to the Holocaust imposed itself on my mind as I walked out of Madison Square Garden. Her giant hanging covered the whole wall of one of the big rooms adjacent to the conference. Why would the destruction of European Jewry become the centerpiece of what it means to be Jewish in America? I kept asking myself over and over.

"What's so amazing about it?" Joe asked, looking bemusedly at the World Trade Center out the window, when I told him about the conference and the statement of the young man from Seattle.

"At first, I thought it was said in jest—a sick joke—you know, our self-deprecating humor. I just couldn't believe that we have turned our misfortune into a ritual and are worshipping a state. It seems sick, perverse!" Still looking out the window, Joe's face was now shadowed by reservation. He was hearing me, but I had a feeling that he was drifting away, I was not reaching him. "Can I run it by you from the beginning?" I asked.

"Go ahead."

"Imagine the conference as a dream," I said. The light of bemusement returned to his face (he wrote a book about the interpretation of dreams). "You are on a train racing through the night. Bombs are going off everywhere. Finally the train is screeching on the rails, coming to a stop. You climb out of the wreckage. There is no train or locomotive, all that was of the train ahead is gone. The car is on a bridge, half of it gone. You make your way back, one crossbar to the next. Underneath is the river. Around you, people take off into the night. You come upon a big building, a steel and glass world. Looking down from the ceiling is a giant plastic replica of the old yellow star, bright with lights. At the center of the room is the old train, faithfully recreated. It is all there, in quadraphonic echoes coming from high-tech speakers in the walls, from the whistles of the bombs before they hit the targets, to the mayhem, smell of fear, desperation, the clawing at the air. And for the last touch to the "You Are There" at a moment in history, the defining moment, someone with a fifty-year long stick is there pointing where to put the dots on the Is and cross the Ts. He was still shaking his head when I left him.

New York, 1988

My sign read, "Stop the killing in Jerusalem." I took it to the local synagogue. On arriving, the rabbi, seeing me holding it up, stopped me and said, "You are wasting your time here. Go to the one on Fifth Avenue, you will do more good there." So on Saturday morning, I planted myself with my sign at the entrance of New York's Fifth Avenue Synagogue, a pillar of mainstream Jewish cultural life.

On seeing me, most members looked the other way. I could hear children's voices: "Why is this man here? What is he protesting . . . ?" as they were being dragged away. A few members just mumbled something under their breath as they passed me by. Some hissed. A few called me "traitor!" One young man spat on me and one actually came over and asked, "Why are you protesting? There is a meeting this evening," he said, "at another synagogue, to discuss our 'Reclamation Project.'"

"What is the 'Reclamation Project?'" I asked.

"It is an organized effort to buy land and property from Palestinians in the occupied territories," he said. He asked if I would be interested in addressing his congregation.

"I will be there," I said.

"I heard about your 'Reclamation Project' this morning," I told the congregation, after he introduced me. "I have been thinking about it all day. To be perfectly honest, it troubles me. I thought it best to come and share my thoughts with you." Members interrupted me angrily, demanding to know if I was Jewish. Others turned to their rabbi, demanding to know who gave this man permission to speak. "We don't have to listen to him, he doesn't even look Jewish," someone kept repeating at the top of his voice. I was astounded at their reaction, I thought they would at least wait until I had said something.

I went on, telling them about Alfons Goldmann, my grandfather, who in 1938 was forced to sell his house and department store in Rosswein. "All these years," I said, "I thought it was an act of theft. I expect the German government will some day return the house to me. What I found troubling about your Reclamation Project is how do you justify it, without justifying the forced sale of my grandfather's property in 1938?

"Anti-Semite! . . . Traitor," they shouted, banging the tables in a fury, desperate to be noticed. "Stop this man!" "How dare you!" "This is an outrage!" "We don't have to listen to this . . ." "Stop him! Stop him!" They were shouting at the rabbi.

My time was running out, I had to make my point fast. "Your Reclamation Project does to us what Hitler tried, but failed to do. You are conceding a victory to Hitler in death that he never achieved in life." That did it. The room blew up. The rabbi was on his feet now, waving his arms in the air: "Please, please! I am sorry . . . Please!" He was like a traffic cop, desperately waving his arms in the face of an oncoming pileup. "I am sorry," he kept shouting, repeating himself over and over until, miraculously, he could finally be heard. "Time does not permit us to go on with this discussion any further," he said. "I would like to introduce our guest speaker of the evening, our acquisition agent in Israel."

He was an American boy in a Brooks Brothers suit with tightly cropped hair and wire-rim glasses. He gave a businesslike account of properties bought, prices paid, properties "under negotiations" and properties targeted for acquisitions down the road. After a brief period in which he answered questions about current "market value," mortgage rates, and security problems (which with a wave of the hand and a smile he assured them was no problem). I had had enough. I walked out.

As I was leaving, a few members came after me, tugging at my sleeves, telling me what they would do to a rock-throwing Palestinian if they got half a chance. One member grabbed me by the shirt, his face alight with fury, waving a fist in my face and said, "Every one of them that raises a rock should be killed! On the spot! I would do no less to my own children if they as much as dared to lift a stone. To be Jewish," he spewed in my face, "is to take an eye for an eye!" He was a milk-fed kid with hardly a whisker.

Whose eye was he talking about, I wondered, walking home in the rain. And then Santayana's lines came to mind: "One must always, without necessarily being a pessimist, be prepared for the worst. for the end of what we call our western civilization and all that grandeur of Christian romanticism . . . We are sailing ever deeper into the dark, uncharted waters. The lights in the lighthouse are beginning to go out. Is there anything to guide us? Is there anyone worth listening to? I wake up in the middle of the night and I am cold with terror . . ."

Looking at my doorman in the lobby from the other side of the street, I felt for the first time like a stranger peering out at my home from an old far away life.

I was speechless when Beverly asked me how it went. The scene at the synagogue was like fireworks, exploding without sound into clouds of colorful smoke suspended over the head of the congregation. I could not describe what took place . . . .

On a nature program that evening, a herd of buffalos, gazelles, and antelopes were caught by cameras, stampeding across the Kalahari Desert. From the air, from trucks on the ground, cameras followed the herd all the way until it vanished over a cliff.

I went to bed with that earth-shaking sound in my head. In the middle of the night, I woke up with the kid's fist in my face and the sound of the herd, stampeding to oblivion, and I saw the congregation, frenzied, swords in hand, charging ahead, avenging themselves on history.

I never stopped to think that a reclamation project run out of a Manhattan synagogue in 1988 might not be news when I called Anthony Lewis at the *New York Times*. "I thought you might want to write about it," I said. He was sympathetic and suggested that I write it instead. I did. He seemed to like the piece and suggested I take it down to Forty-third Street. He did what he could to get it published, but the *Times* rejected my piece as "inappropriate," as did the *Washington Post*.

To reveal the essence of the message commercial photographers use white reflectors and black flags. White reflectors to eliminate unwanted shadows and black flags to tone down unwanted light reflected on the subject. In other words they manipulate the message by manipulating the light.

Disappointed and angry, I called Lewis. "You are too harsh on them," he said on the phone when I expressed my disappointment. And, of course, he was right. I was harsh, out of step with the times. Worse yet, I was naive to think it was also newsworthy just because I thought it was significant. In truth, it was probably neither. It wasn't newsworthy because even though America's Jews remained silent, most were embarrassed by Israel's response to the Intifada. It did not fit with the Israel they worshiped. And it was not significant because the embarrassment American Jews felt was not about Israel but about themselves. After 1967, most put their hearts, their Jewish identity and many of their dollars in the Israel basket and were thrilled to do so. What they never counted on was that one day a dim-witted Prime Minister would pick it all up and run away with it, first into Lebanon, and now into an occupied land, in search of redemption.

Whatever remained of the feeling of pride after 1967 was buried in the rubble of Beirut, Lebanon. The first stone of the Intifada fractured the mirror, that magic mirror of Jewish identity that American Jews saw themselves in every morning as they shaved or put on their makeup. Only the lunatic Right could identify with Israeli soldiers clubbing and shooting Palestinian children.

New York, 1990

At the last Passover we were invited to in New York, the host who conducted the seder drove through the sections of "remembering the Holocaust . . . and thanking God that we are a free people, in a free land" without taking his foot off the gas. Even though an hour earlier Israeli soldiers were on his

TV screen beating Palestinians. We recited the same old phrases from the same old books, worn out by time and use. The young asked the same old questions, while the grown-ups, if they had any, drowned them in chicken soup.

Antibes, France, June 1990

My dear Mugwump,*

I was on my way to our last breakfast together in New York. You were seventeen. I had hoped until the last moment to find some way to explain to you why I was leaving America, but words failed me, as they do when I really need them. I was lost in a cloud of guilt—how little time we had together, what it must be for you, growing up with an absent father. All I could say to you was that my life in America no longer makes sense. It has become unbearable.

Three incidents during my first week in America stand out as omens, unheeded at the time, but as relevant today as they were then.

I was on the Holland American Line's *Maasdam* on the twenty-second of November 1963. It was approaching U.S. territorial waters when the news came over the public address system that President Kennedy had been shot. The second shift lunchers, mostly Europeans, were visibly shaken by shock and disbelief. The announcement that the president was dead came sometime later, followed by a notice that the afternoon movie would be cancelled and that the shop's bar would be closed. On deck near the bar there was a commotion. A group of Americans, mostly Texans and Oklahomans, were protesting the closing, saying that they wanted to celebrate, and as paying passengers, they could insist on their rights. A voice came over the loud speaker, "This is your captain. The bar will stay closed. If the American passengers wish to complain they may do so to the authorities in New York."

The next morning, after my first night in New York, handgun shots rang out as I was coming down the stairs of my friend's apartment at 47th Street and Ninth Avenue. A determined Chinese man was standing in the doorway of his laundry. He came up to

---

*   Peter's pet name for his daughter, Lyrissa, who lives in California with his former wife, Luba.

me saying, "No go. No go." He bodily dragged me to his window overlooking the street. There, on the stoop, was a man lying motionless in a pink puddle. People, on their way to work, gave him a passing look and kept on walking. As though it was perfectly normal.

Three days later at a Thanksgiving dinner I was invited to, I asked the hostess, "Where are your children? I thought they were in New York."

"They are," she said.

"Then why aren't they here?"

"They are at work."

"On Thanksgiving Day? I thought it was the most important holiday in America?"

"It is," she said. "But in America nothing is more important than the job."

I understood what she meant, but I did not understand its significance until twenty-seven years later, watching America's "high-tech slaughter show" in my living room in Nice. An American pilot, having just returned from a bombing mission over Baghdad, was asked for his impression by a reporter. He responded by saying, "I was just doing my job." I remembered when I had first heard this sentence. It was uttered by Eichmann, tlhe man in the glass booth.[*]

I am still hardly able to think of you without being conscious of the pain your absence will generate, but I knew, too, that I cannot go on living in America. I hope that reading these notes will in some way be of help to you.

LOVE, DAD

Leaving New York was a major step. I was twenty-five when I arrived, with a pair of dance slippers in an overnight flight bag. I had lived here for twenty-seven years, longer then I had lived anywhere. Leaving New York was, though I didn't realize it until two years later, more of an uprooting than a move or a departure.[**]

---

[*]   Adolf Eichmann, enclosed in a protective glass booth during his 1961 trial in Israel for his role in the "Final Solution."

[**] Peter and Beverly moved to the South of France in July of 1990, staying for the first few months in her apartment in Antibes.

CHAPTER 4

THE ASSIGNMENT

PETER PAZ
Le Belvedere, Blvd. James Willy, Antibes, France, 06600

FAX TO: MR. HJ*
RECHTSANWALT UND NOTAR
JULY 8, 1990

Dear Mr. HJ:*

I will be traveling on assignment in Europe in August (Budapest, Prague, Berlin, and Leipzig). I would like very much to see you in Berlin.

I plan to apply for citizenship in East Germany and explore the state and status of the property my grandparents left me.

I will be arriving in Berlin August 20 and plan to stay until the 29, or later if need be. If that time frame is inconvenient for you please let me know when you could meet with me.

Looking forward to seeing you.

Yours sincerely,
Peter Paz

---

* For the purposes of this publication, the lawyers who represented Peter for the reclamation of his grandfather's property are identified by initials, not necessarily their own. The complete correspondence can be found in the Peter Paz file housed at the Baeck Institute in New York. See chapter notes.

Budapest, August 1990

I was at the Zurich airport when I learned of Iraq's invasion of Kuwait. I was on my way to Berlin on a photo assignment, but to collect myself, Beverly and I decided to spend the weekend in Budapest.

Starting out from the old Gellert Hotel before sunrise, I crossed the bridge over to Pest, heading for Budapest's old train station on the bank of the Danube, an unforgettable stop of the old Orient Express, now converted into an indoor market. Inside, beams of yellow-orange light filtered through the skylight windows illuminating the pale faces of vendors and shoppers, moving slowly in a semidusty gray darkness, damp with a sharp scent of fermenting fruit, vegetables, fresh flowers, and broken promises.

In the old days, shooting surreptitiously here would have generated resentment and I would have been ordered to leave at once. This morning, a pall of resignation hung over the place. Stealing their images with a camera mounted on a three-foot high tripod generated neither resentment nor curiosity. No one seemed to notice me. Around noontime, I gave in to fatigue and tradition and parked myself at one of Budapest's old Austro-Hungarian Empire-time cafés. At the next table, a group of Germans from the last war were loudly debating the coming one. On the other side, two Americans were talking about it with a table of Israelis, who sounded confident, even eager for this war. Everyone, it seems, was represented in that room of nostalgia: the French, the Arabs, the Japanese, the Russians, and the Poles. A tired old Gypsy band played on in the smoke as former enemies, perpetrators, victims, collaborators, and spectators all perfectly behaved, sat around sipping coffee and munching on cake topped with "schlag," warming themselves up in three-quarter time for another round.

Two women, decked out in gold, diamonds and Italy's latest, talking a mile a minute in Polish, asked to join my table in a heavily accented English. With what was on their backs and fingers they could have pulled Poland's economy out of its ashes. My curiosity got the better of me and in my accented English I asked,

"Are you from Poland?"

"Not really," they said, "we are from Israel."

"And how is Israel these days?" I asked, after recovering from my surprise.

"Oh, it is better than ever. You should come and see it, we have everything now, anything you can get in New York, we can now get in Tel Aviv or Haifa," said the one with the diamonds.

"Then what, if you don't mind me asking, are you doing in Budapest?"

"Well," said the one who was in gold, "we are on vacation."

"In Budapest, in August?" I asked.

"Well," she said, "it doesn't really matter to us where, we just get away every six months."

I told them that I grew up in a kibbutz by the sea, but had not been back to Israel in twenty-five years.

"Oh, you will not recognize it if you will come to Israel now," said the one with the diamonds, without missing a beat.

"Are you worried about Iraq?" I asked.

"How can we not be worried?" said the diamond lady. "We are always worried, never far from a radio. To worry is a way of life in Israel, and that is why I have to get away every six months. If I didn't, I would go crazy."

*   *   *

My assignment in Berlin was to create an image centered around a Goodyear service truck, (actually a Mercedes Benz van, the kind used in New York to deliver diapers and bagels), for the company's Annual Report. At first, the PR Department in Akron suggested using the Berlin Wall as a backdrop. But by the time I arrived in Berlin, the wall was history. The Department was now pushing the Brandenburg Gate as a backdrop of choice for their little service van. To make up for its insignificant size, they suggested that if I used the magic of a wide-angle lens on the little van, it could be made to look bigger than the Brandenburg Gate.

For the rebirth of Germany united (not the Fourth Reich, I kept repeating to myself), the man and beasts on top of the Brandenburg Gate, who had been gazing down at the Germans as they lost two wars and managed to come out ahead, had been taken off to the cleaners. I suspected that the idea of the gate, now naked, would not fly back in Akron, Ohio. And indeed, I was off the hook. There were no more ideas from Akron. After much scouting throughout the DDR, I selected a little square in Weimar, with a detour to Guttern as an alternative for the little Goodyear service van.

Set in a sea of August wheat, Guttern's some thirty houses are huddled around a silent church. From a nearby hilltop, I had the entire village in my lens. Apart from a man who was shoveling manure onto a broken down trailer and a dog resting in the shade, Guttern seemed deserted. The single evident soul accentuated the emptiness of this Brueghel-like landscape. An oppressive sky of brown soot, smog, and humidity hung overhead, going nowhere. If, however, by chance, the sun were to break through, the little Goodyear van would be immortalized in a blazing, Van Gogh-like setting. I decided to wait. After a couple of hours on top of the hill, I gave up. My commitment to "corporate art" was defeated by heat, thirst, and by the fact that it was a Saturday in the DDR. At the stroke of noon, the entire country zips up. And nothing reopens before Monday morning. Waiting for my Van Gogh fantasy on top of this hill meant staying thirsty and hungry until well into the night, when with a little luck, I could be back in West Berlin. I settled for the deserted, muddy Brueghel and was on my way, racing at a breakneck speed against a German clock, anticipating all the way to Eisenbach, the fizz of an cold Coke trickling down my dry throat.

It was five minutes past twelve. In the shadow of the town's tallest church, a yellow barbecue trailer was still open. A Middle Eastern looking character was offering warm Coke and cold sausages, with a straight face. Stefan, my driver, who saw my percolating indignation, stopped me, reminding me that a fifteen-minute drive past Eisenbach would bring us to the border. On the West German side, we would find all the cold Coke and warm food we could take in. I hesitated because rain clouds were moving in the direction of Weimar. Going for the Coke meant the rain might get to Weimar before we did. Stefan, who had been driving the van all day as if the Stasi (DDR's secret police) was after him, said that if there were no police, we would probably make it. I figured that since the DDR was already closed down, there was no one to watch. Everyone would be at home, so the police would be where everyone else was. So I went for the Coke, Stefan flying the little van over ancient potholes at 110 miles per hour.

Once a proud repository of German Humanistic tradition, Weimar stands today perfectly preserved in the shadow of Buchenwald. It was here from the balcony of the Elephant Hotel, in the heart of Luther's country, that Adolf Hitler preached the Gospel of National Socialism to God-fearing Sunday crowds of ordinary, every-day law-abiding decent people. Before him, Goethe wrote *Faust* here. Herder, Schiller, Kandinsky, Edmund Husserl, and Paul Klee all lived and worked here.

Heavy clouds were gathering in on Weimar when we arrived. The town square, ringed by yellow-orange houses, was slipping slowly into twilight. By the time I finished setting-up, a fine drizzle was coming down, cooling off the sunbaked cobblestones, filling the empty square with a musky smell of summer, laced with the dust of local history. Through the camera, I saw an elderly woman looking down at me from a second floor window. Behind me a group of beer-drinking skinheads, getting high on "Deutschland uber alles," were not amused by my presence and kept shouting "*keine foto namen, foto verbotten! foto verbotten! auslander raus! Raus!*" I got my shot, packed the car, and was off, the metallic sound of "Deutschland uber alles" following me into the darkness.

Back at the Heidelberger Hotel, I was debating with myself: Should I go look up the house in Rosswein or skip it? Grandfather left it to me in his will, and it was in the flight from this house that my mother and I lost each other.

It was getting late. Christian, Stefan's younger brother, was coming with his car before daybreak to drive us there. I could not call him too late if I changed my mind about going. I was riding a roller coaster in two directions at the same time. In my head one was Mildred's* voice: "You are the hero of your own movie." Suddenly, a new window materialized in an opaque wall, as if by the magic of a word. Here was my chance, I thought. After fifty-two years of hiding, I can redeem myself, become the hero of my movie. All I have to do is go back to the house where I was born** and where the ghosts of my past are.

I decided to go, mostly, because the spectre of turning back loomed like a shadow more ominous than the ghosts residing in my grandfather's old house, following me for the rest of my days. So on the morning of my fifty-second birthday, I set out with Beverly for the house in Rosswein.

Monday morning, anticipating long lines at the Office of Records, Christian picked us up before Berlin's first cafes opened. At eight o'clock sharp, we were in the lobby of the district archives at Boden, a massive 18th century building covered by the standard layer of east German soot. Gray marble circular steps led us to the second floor. Room B25, the Office of Records, was halfway down a long unlit corridor. On the door was a handwritten note that had been written a long time ago saying "Office open Tuesday and Wednesday from 10-2, closed Thursday and Friday, inquiries in room #B26." On the door of #B26 was a note saying "Closed Monday to Thursday, open Friday 14-17, inquiries at room #B27." The note at #B27 in the same handwriting said, "Office closed! Inquire in room #B25." Astonished, we stared at each other in disbelief. We followed Christian downstairs to regroup. About halfway down, we saw a woman rushing across the floor. Christian took after her, his foot was in the door before she could close it. When she realized it, she just blurted out, "What do you want? I don't know anything, it has nothing to do with me!" Fortunately, Christian had a healthy disrespect for authority, he

---

* Mildred Newman, Peter's group therapy co-leader with Joe Katz
** See chapter notes concerning where Peter was born.

kept his foot in the door and persisted in questioning her, which finally made her say, "The office upstairs is not closed, you must go back. Knock and keep knocking! Keep knocking! There are people behind all the doors. It is all one office. You must keep knocking, but please don't tell them that I told you."

After a few rounds of our serious knocking, a disheveled, oversized clerk opened the door, irritated and out of breath. He looked like he had slept in his clothes. His pants, held up by a cracked cardboard belt, were about to surrender momentarily to his beer belly. His eyes were dark and lifeless, bulging as he barked, "We are closed," pointing to the note on the door. Christian explained that we had come all the way from New York to see him and must go back to New York tomorrow. He must have realized that we were not going to go away quietly. He barked in the same tone, "You must wait!" and closed the door in our face.

We settled in for a long wait on the un-upholstered bench facing room B25. A single window was the only source of light in this quiet, clean, gray marble corridor. I told Christian how impressed I was by his performance downstairs. "All clerks," I said, "are vulnerable. The more rigid the system the more vulnerable they are. To get anything from them they must be leaned on and shaken, like a tree."

Two men wearing blue coats and rubber-soled shoes came out from one of the offices, carrying a huge square wicker basket, overflowing with fat little packets of files, each neatly tied with butcher's string. Looking straight ahead, they walked silently in step past our bench; and in silence, we watched them disappear down the stairs. A while later they reappeared from the same office that they left a few minutes before, carrying the same wicker basket. They walked by us, still in step, looking straight ahead, and we watched them disappear again down the gray marble steps.

Finally the clerk reappeared at the door and beckoned us to come in. The room smelled of preserved papers. I felt like I had stepped into a world that did not have a floor. I was sinking. Sinking in time. I saw myself sitting there, helpless, waiting for some evidence of a past I never fully accepted. Actually thinking at one point that the clerk would come back and say, "There has been a mistake, there is no file, it never existed." But the clerk was back, spreading an 1881 map of Rosswein's properties in front of me. He found my grandfather's house in less than a minute. In less than another minute, his assistant brought out the file of the house.

As I was staring at his handwriting on the piece of paper lying in front of me, an image of my grandfather, of whom I had no memory or picture, began to form itself in my mind. He had a textile shop in Rosswein until 1937 when he was forced to hand it over to one Bruno Max Taubert, a Nazi party member, whose handwriting was next to my grandfather's. After handing over the house, he was taken to the Leipzig Ghetto, where he lived for fifteen months shoveling snow in the winter and sweeping the street in the summer. Alfons Goldmann was seventy-eight years old and in good health when he was taken to Theresinstadt, where he died. I was not quite there while all of this was going on, the ghosts that were once a part of my life were holding me under a spell.

Beverly, without whom I would probably not have taken this journey, took down the name of the present registered owner, and we were done. We were on the street in less than ten minutes. Walking us to the door, the clerk said in German, thinking we would not understand, "I wish that the floodgates will open and drown Rosswein and everyone in it."

Later, on the road to Rosswein, the scene in the office hung suspended in the silence of the car, unresolved. At first I thought that the speed in which the clerk came up with the map and file of the house was perhaps due to many of Rosswein's surviving Jews who were there before me. But there was a personal sound in his last remark that kept ringing in my mind as we came closer to Rosswein. "Could the clerk," I asked myself, "have known my grandfather?" While in Berlin, I came upon two depositions at my lawyers, taken in 1961, testifying to my grandfather's character, his store, health, spirit, and the date of his deportation. From the deposition, it was clear that one of the witnesses visited my grandfather in the Leipzig Ghetto. That witness was a tenant in my grandfather's house and a clerk in that very Office of Records. Was the clerk in his office speaking to the ghost of Alfons Goldmann?

The smell of golden ripe wheat evoked memories of my mother that have not faded through the years. In the first, my mother and I were having a picnic on top of a hill under a huge tree. I remember the sun shining through, the leaves appearing like transparent spots of green and yellow light moving gently in the sky. In the second, I am holding on to my mother's hand, running through an endless sea of golden ripe wheat to Leipzig, where the Gestapo caught up with us and turned us in.

It was past ten in the morning when we arrived. Rosswein's sunny side of the street was as gray and dark as was the side of the street in the shade. The whole town was smothered in bleakness. The streets were empty. The stores were closed. We went directly to Mulenstrasse. Over the front door of the house under a layer of grime was the original 1901 "Kaufhaus" sign of grandfather Alfons's store. It was now a plumber's workshop. I entered the house feeling like a ghost, wandering through it in slow motion, silently, as not to miss a clue that might jar my sleeping memory. A struggling plant stood by a window on the second floor's landing, casting a soft shadow on two cases of empty bottles of beer and bricks of coal in a bucket. In the corner of my eye, I caught a glimpse of a face retreating behind a silently closing door. I left the house in a state of numbness, unable to feel, defeated by the hard-core center of detachment that for many years kept me going. Walking to the car, I noticed faces peering out from windows and doorways. The eyes followed me long after the car turned the corner and the house on Mulenstrasse disappeared from view. It was then that I realized that for the most part, I had been living as a tourist in my own life. I had been staring in the mirror, and it was empty.

We stopped for lunch at an old hotel and restaurant at the edge of town. The smell in the place, the light coming through the old yellow lace curtains, the wallpaper, tablecloth, waitress, and diners in this smoke-filled room were like faded pictures from an old family album. In the car heading back to Berlin, still feeling haunted by how familiar and homelike this place felt, I heard myself thinking, "What would my life have been like? Had it all been a dream?" I shuddered at the thought.

FAX TO: HJ, September 1990

Dear HJ:

I first want to thank you for taking the time from what was obviously a busy day for you to see me. You were as gracious and as generous as I remembered you to be when we first met way back in 1963.

Your advice and information about the property in Rosswein was accurate and most helpful.

Here is the information you requested:

The House in Rosswein: 18 Muhlstrase:

* The property is 270 square meters. The front house is 3 stories high. In the back there is another house that is 2 stories high and about 20 meters long. It has at least one tenant.
* The front house is in very good condition and is fully occupied. It faces a street that is a mix of commercial and residential properties.

* The ground floor is a plumber's workshop.
* The upper-floors are rented. Ginter (the present owner) lives in the second—floor apartment facing the street. The third floor seems to be rented to a party named Fuchs.

The following are the registered owners of the house at 18 Muhlstrasse
1901: Alfons Goldmann owned 50% of the property.
1907: Alfons Goldmann owned 100% of the property.
1937-1945: Bruno Max Taubert
1945-1974: Taubert's widow, B. Seifert, remarried Mr. Loeffler and the property was registered under his name.
1974-to the present: Erich Ginter

While Rudolf Goldmann* was in Israel in 1961 he came to visit me for the purpose of obtaining a signature from me. I do not remember what the particular document was, whether I signed it or whether it was in English or in Hebrew. All I remember is that I was quite stunned and apprehensive because 16 years after the end of the war, during which I had heard not a single word from my uncle, he appeared. I have not heard from him since. Needless to say, I am most interested in the document in question.

If you have the document, would you please examine it and advise me whether or not I may have compromised my interests and what course of action, if any, you recommend.

Let me know if there is anything you required regarding my application for German citizenship.

Best regards,
Peter Paz

---

* brother of Peter's mother, who immigrated to Australia with his wife and daughter in the 1930s

PART II

Nice: 1990-2001

CHAPTER 5

LIFE IN PARADISE

Antibes, France, 1990

Under the blazing Mediterranean sun, from this balcony hanging over the water, the eye can roam unobstructed all the way up to the Alps now capped with snow. Below it, Nice is pleasuring itself in the deep blues of Matisse. In the mornings as I walk by the sea, I often find myself wandering off, back to Rosswein, where demons, ghosts, and echoes of rage still hang, unclaimed, in the air. When I emerge, I find myself here, walking through these narrow alleyways of ancient stone, perfumed by this gentle sea. It is an unlikely setting for reflections on a life lived in the shadow of Rosswein, but I could not imagine one that is better, or as Beverly says, "More just."

Antibes, September 1990

Dear Joe:

I haven't stopped writing since my return from Rosswein. Shuttling between the past and the Cote d'Azur, there are moments when I feel that I am digging a hole for myself. It's getting deeper. Every time I look up I see less of the sky then I did the last time I looked. At times I wonder "why?" Why re-create a life that has been forgotten, faded away into the infinite space of forgetting?

Life, as I always suspected, is much like a house one turns into a home by living in it, tending the garden, mending the roof, the cracks in the walls, washing the windows, letting the air in. It is unique though, in that it can't be sold, traded, moved out of or abandoned, without sooner or later afflicting the owner by the sense of being homeless, lost.

For as long as I can remember, I took to the notion that the past was the past, it couldn't be changed, so why not let it be, like an old suitcase up in the attic, packed with clothes that no longer are fashionable, and forget all about it?

Growing up among "the children of the dream," life was about the future. Everyone was into dreaming of a future, a different future, a future as far away as possible from our past. Forgetting was not only convenient, it was the only accepted way. Only now, from the distance of time, am I able to ask myself, "What did it feel like, growing up in an extended family, with twenty-two brothers and sisters and more then two hundred uncles and aunts, and not be asked even once, "Where did you come from? What was it like over there? How do you feel?"

It wasn't until I walked through the silent corridors of the house in Rosswein that I was struck by how empty I felt being there. I had forgotten. I had disappeared.

The problem with remembering is that it is pretty much like the baby and the bath water. Memory can't be disposed of selectively. It took a long time before the irony of "forgetting all about it" took shape in my mind. I was reading the notes of my visit to Weimar when the bells struck. Just as it was impossible to be in Weimar and not be struck by the richness of its past, it was equally impossible to comprehend how Weimar, with its humanist's tradition, ended up living in the shadow of Buchenwald.

The only buffer between Weimar and Buchenwald was the past, what people remembered. It was there, in the mirror of the past, that they saw indulging mothers; stern, unyielding fathers; grandmothers and grandfathers who spoiled them rotten and talked about life, their joys, music, books, laughter, celebrations, love, old friends, heartbreak, fear, humiliation, pain, defeat, despair, death and perseverance.

It was there that the people of Weimar got the sense of who they were and what made Weimar Weimar. And it was that memory that the National Socialists had to overcome, discredit, erase, obliterate, before they could begin building Buchenwald.

It has been our lot that we have least of the former and most of the latter, but through it all and in spite of it, we held on, we remembered who we were, we remained Human. What are we, after all, but what we remember? Forgetting, then, is nothing less than the slow voluntary march toward self-destruction.

The race to forget had been on long before Ronald Reagan, the president of forgetting, journeyed to Bitburg.* We may look at it as a bit of History's whimsy or as a prophetic act, ushering in an age where forgetting is not just the main thing, it's the only thing.

If "the struggle of man against power is the struggle of memory against forgetting" as Mirek says in Milan Kundera's *The Book of Laughter and Forgetting*, then Weimar today is a monument to the triumph of power and the defeat of memory. A monument to darkness, casting its long shadow on all of us.

How did forgetting prevail? Remembering was the only worthwhile lesson we of this century could have passed on to the next. Looking around these days, I fear that we have failed.

I hope these somewhat somber musings find you well in body and spirit and that you will forgive me for not having written sooner.

Give my love to Mildred and the Group. I miss them all sorely.

I am looking eagerly to your coming.

Love, Peter

Nice, France, January 10, 1991

My dear Mugwump:

Since returning from Rosswein, I have been trying unsuccessfully to shed some light on my new life. I hope you will forgive me for taking so long to write you. I write slowly, but mostly, it is that much of what has been on my mind since I left New York is taking a long time to sort out. Too much has been happening too fast. Throughout the trip to Budapest, Prague, and all the way to

---

* In 1985, during the commemoration of the fortieth anniversary of the Second World War, President Reagan made a stop at the military cemetery in Bitberg, Germany. He drew criticism for laying a wreath where Nazi SS soldiers were buried.

Rosswein, where I found my grandfather's house frozen in time, I have been recalling the image of you greeting me on camp's visiting day as a way of lighting some of the darker passages of my journey. Only after my return to Antibes did I realize that the journey to Rosswein was the easy part, coming back will take some time.

I miss talking to you and feel very badly at not being able to get the French telephone company to fix the problem with my American phone. They say that I should get a French one. I will be moving to Nice at the end of the month, so hopefully I won't have the same problem there.

Just as I thought this letter was finished, we found an apartment in the old Italian section of Nice, at the port. We moved on Christmas Eve and as of this writing are still camping in it, with a second-hand stove, a refrigerator, a mattress on the floor and a photographic light stand for a night lamp. It is a sunny, spacious apartment in the heart of the most fabulous neighborhood. As we walk through, we catch ourselves simultaneously thinking the same thought, "we actually live here, it's not a dream." There are three patisseries on our block, two butchers, four restaurants, five cafes, a Chinese laundry, a Chinese restaurant, a cut-rate furniture store, two antique furniture places, and a four-screen movie house. The Museum of Modern Art and Nice's theater are across the square, and down the block, the Old City's food, fish and flower market, which on Mondays is turned into a giant market for antiques. It will be our permanent home. We will have the guest room finished by this summer and look forward to your coming.

Love, Dad

Nice, France, May 16, 1991

Dear Joe:

For the first time in my life, I knew someone who was in a position to give me a break, professionally. It actually saved me from spending the summer selling jewelry in the Nice market. Instead, I spent the summer traveling around Europe, shooting a series of ads that introduced "Eurocopter" to the business world at the Paris air show. It is a joint French-German company made up of the infamous German Messerschmidt Company and Aerospatiale of France, France's largest helicopter company.

When the art director* called me from Paris, he said that he'd fax me a series of portraits by Richard Avedon and Arnold Newman, saying that that was what the client was looking for. Could I do it? It is the first year since I became a photographer that I haven't had a job in the season. Was it the Gulf War or my move to France? A desperate voice in me whispered, "You can do it, you can do it." So I said, "I can do it."

I told Bill that the most sensible way to handle this was for me to come to Paris to shoot a test. And since these were to be no ordinary portraits, I asked him to set up a dinner with the subject, an executive of Aerospatiale, so that I could get to know him before I was to shoot him. I booked myself on the overnight train that very day . . . .**

---

*   Bill Chevallier, husband of Beverly's cousin, Sheila Malovany-Chevallier
**   Peter got the job and spent the next several months on location.

CHAPTER 6

FRANKFURT-BERLIN JOURNAL

Nice, September 25, 1991

Dear Joe:

I spent most of July in Paris, printing out my portfolio and looking for an agent. Lyrissa came in August for a 10-day stay. It was the best of visits. Julie* came for the last week of August, but we did not see much of her. That's the way Julie's visits have always been. She applied for and got accepted by the film school in Paris.

At the beginning of September I took my newly printed portfolio to Frankfurt to look for an agent. On arrival, I went to the old Palace Hotel, a comfortable place on the edge of Frankfurt's red light district and within walking distance from the train station. The night clerk, a recently arrived refugee from Macedonia, informed me that there was a convention in town and that the hotel was full. My friend, the Polish expatriate manager, was no longer with the hotel. But, he said, "I'll try and find you a room for the night. Come back after dinner." I left my luggage and went back to the station to have dinner and a few beers. Eating and drinking in the company of wanderers, people in transit, immigrants, and people on their way down or out, made me feel both more at home and, disturbingly, more displaced. I berated myself for not having called ahead to reserve, and then, in compensation, over-ate. I had used the Palace as a home away from home ever since my first shooting assignment in Frankfurt, more than twenty

---

*   Beverly's daughter

years ago. When I returned to the hotel, the clerk had a room for me at the Hotel Terminus across the street. "It was the only room I could find that was not way out of town," he said. The room turned out to be a converted utility room, well-heated, with a sink, telephone, and a TV. What more can one ask in a cold wet night in Frankfurt? I turned on the TV and went under the covers. A moderator was just introducing a panel of German, Palestinian and Jewish intellectuals. He concluded the introductions by saying that the Israelis invited to take part in this evening's discussion had declined the invitation because Israel forbids its citizens any contact with members or associates of the PLO. It turned into a heated discussion about the injustice of the occupation, the Palestinian uprising, the threat of a Palestinian state to Israel's security, and promises made by the Almighty.

I drifted off into a dream while the panel kept slugging it out. For the first time since she was taken out of the Gestapo cell, my mother appeared in my dream. My head was resting on her cleavage, I was looking up at her face; her expression was of striking lightness and peace. The panel was still at it when I woke up. I turned the TV off and fell asleep under the glow of her face in the light.

First thing in the morning, I called HJ, my lawyer in Berlin, thinking that there might be some news about the house in Rosswein. He turned me over to his assistant, WM, who spoke a better English. WM suggested that I get in touch with my cousins in Australia to work out "your differences." I told him that since I did not know a thing about my uncle or his children, their names, or even how many children Uncle Rudolf had, I suggested that the two of us first have a meeting on the subject. "But tomorrow is my last day in the office," he said, "I am going on vacation." I persisted and he relented. We agreed to meet at his office the next day at 3:00. When I finally arrived, schlepping my portfolio and luggage, I was 50 minutes late. "What happened to your trains?" I asked him, half in jest. Without missing a beat he said, "It is only trains from the East that are late, the rest of our trains are on time." He said it with a half smile reserved for special occasions, when one talks about voices coming from the attic or to a retarded child. So much for being philosophical about "the new Germany" I said to myself.

HJ, my urban middle-aged lawyer, was wearing a light beige linen suit and a permanent suntan. Back in law school days of old Berlin, his father and Uncle Rudolf were friends. He apologized for not being able to stay, as he was due in court. Turning me over to his assistant, WM, he introduced me as if I was a miraculously preserved fragile parchment. Uncle Rudolf, it turned out, had set out on his final journey some time ago. However, one of his last acts before departing was to leave the Rosswein house to his children, even though grandfather, in his will, had left half of the house to my mother. His children asked no questions and filed a claim for it.

The assistant, WM, in his thirties, of a slight build, was wearing a brown corduroy jacket (a size too small) over a sportscaster's colorful checkered shirt, knotted by a headlight of a tie. He appeared pale and gaunt under his colorful get-up. He led the way to his office through a huge room full of files. It was like walking through a morgue. Everywhere one looked, there were files piled on top of each other, all the way up to the ceiling. Files covered every inch of the floor, save for a narrow walking passage way. As I walked behind him, watching my steps, I thought about the compulsiveness, discipline and fear it took to keep such records. The thought of what must it be like to be born into this legacy and work in this place flashed through my mind. WM's shoulders were stooped, as if weighed down by this sea of decomposing records, waiting for justice, just blocks away from the resuscitated Reichstag.

Files covered all three tables in his small office. "I can give you only a few minutes because I must take care of all of these before I leave today," he said. Having come to Berlin just to see him, I let the remark pass without comment. I sat down and watched him search through the piles of paper. "This is your file," he said, as he laid it on the desk. I watched him leaf through it, feeling a simmering of resentment and anxiety, as though I was watching him walk through a minefield. It was just a matter of time before he tripped over something that would blow up in my face. There were three folders in front of him, lying on top of each other; they were almost a foot high.

I remember almost nothing of my life before the war ended. I watched him go through one page at a time. "I am looking for your grandfather's will," he said and continued, stopping occasionally to scan a piece of paper that caught his attention. My stomach was in knots. The phone rang. "That was my travel agent, to tell me that my wife called with some last-minute questions. We are going on a safari to Kenya," he said and went back to rifling through the file. He stopped to read a document and lifted his eyes, saying, "There is something here I do not understand. It says here that you and your mother are going to America. Do you know anything about it?" It was as unexpected a piece of news as I could imagine. Chills surged up my spine. I felt heat spreading through my head, my face flushed with throbbing waves of heat.

"I do not," I said.

After reading through it again he said, "This is a copy of a Gestapo document giving your mother and you permission to leave the Third Reich. It says here that your mother was of good character, that she had paid her taxes and the travel charge, and is permitted to leave, and that she is sailing from Hamburg on May 13, 1939 for Havana."

The phone rang again.

"That was my wife again, to tell me that she will check in our baggage and that I should meet her at the boarding gate. Where were we?"

"In Havana," I said.

"Well, it also says here that your mother paid the Hamburg-American Line for two round-trip tickets from Hamburg to Havana, plus a travel charge. What I do not understand is why did your mother buy round-trip tickets? It makes no sense!"

I told him that I knew nothing about it. There was a long silence. He waited for me to speak, but the wheels of my mind just seemed to have come to a stop. I was shrinking, drifting away in a cold fog.

For a while after I left his office, I walked around thinking I should call my old friend Lea at the Jewish Center to set up a meeting for the next day. But the thought of actually calling her took me back to our first meeting. It was the summer of 1963. I had left Israel a day or two earlier. The owners of the pension "De Este" where I was staying in Berlin, both Israelis, gave me her number. When I called her she invited me to a party at her house. They were mostly Israelis, children of German Jews who managed to get out in time. Most were in their twenties. Manfred,

Lea's German boyfriend, was in his forties. At some point I heard myself ask Manfred, "What did you know about the death camps?" Silence spread in the room like a brushfire in August. All eyes were focused on him. He was a jolly, well-to-do producer. The question apparently did not surprise him." I first heard about it while at the Russian front," he said. "After I was wounded, I heard about it again. It seemed like everyone in the hospital knew. I did nothing about it. There was nothing I could do but try not to think about it. What would you have done if you were in my place?"

I remember how flabbergasted I was then by the scene, and by what Manfred had said. Now, almost thirty years later, I was wandering aimlessly through the streets of Charlottenburg, doodling in the dark, filling in the empty spaces with images in slow motion of my mother turning herself inside-out, scurrying from pillar to post to find a way out from a mousetrap that was already shut. The echo of Manfred's voice replayed itself over the blurred images. His words sounded as strikingly true now, as they did then. And then there was the shaking head of WM, sitting behind my file, repeating to himself, "It makes no sense, it just makes no sense!" came and went. The jumbled images would fade away and replay themselves all over again. At some point I noticed the pouring rain. I was soaking wet. I found a phone booth. I stood by the phone, dripping, trying to summon the words to call Lea, but all I could draw was a blank. I called Stefan instead.

He had left Goodyear to open his own car service station in East Berlin. He was working late, which left me time to go back to the Heidelberger Hotel, take a bath and change. I had not seen Stefan since his brother, Christian, drove me to Rosswein more than a year before. Over Chinese food we compared lawyer's stories and talked about his plans to lease a place near Alexanderplatz for another car service station. And about my prospects of recovering the house in Rosswein. I told him that they seemed more remote now than when we first went looking for the house. "Don't give up," he said.

His biggest client in East Berlin was the Russian Embassy, but it was broke and was paying its bills in vodka and caviar. "It is a little bit of a problem," he said sheepishly, "because I am a vegetarian and my apartment is filling up with vodka and caviar."

THE JEWISH CENTER

Berlin, 1988

I was last at the Jewish Center in Berlin in 1984. At that time, it was a place where people came and went freely all hours of the day and into the evening. Now it was a maze of video cameras, bulletproof Plexiglas barriers guarded by aged men sitting in little bulletproof cubicles, armed to the teeth, smoking their last cigarette twenty times a day. On the walls were posters from Israel's National Tourist Office, urging viewers to "Come Visit the Dream," and above them electronic eyes that could count the coins in my pocket. Lea in her office insisted on speaking in Hebrew, but answered her telephone in perfect High German.

There was no archive at the center. Lea suggested that I contact a mutual friend who used to teach at Berlin's Free University. He said he knew of an archive that might have what I was looking for. After some digging, we came upon a file marked "Jewish Immigration from the Third Reich 1933-1940." It was mostly news clippings from German and English newspapers and magazines. There were some clippings from the American press. There was only one ship listed as having left Hamburg with German Jewish Immigrants on board on May 13, 1939. It was the *Saint Louis*.

Excerpt from the Archive:

On Friday, June 2, 1939 at 11 a.m. the *St. Louis* sailed back for Hamburg. Hardened newspapermen in accompanying launches wept openly as hundreds of refugees lined the rails imploring Cuba for mercy and straining for a final sight of loved ones on the dock. At eleven forty on Tuesday evening, June 6, 1939, the *Saint Louis* ended her idle cruising and set her course back to Europe. A committee of passengers addressed a telegram to Franklin D. Roosevelt asking help for 907 passengers, of which 400 were women and children. There was no reply.

Captain Schroeder was delaying his return to Hamburg as long as possible, sailing past Miami, offering his 734 passengers with U.S. Immigration papers a glimpse of their future homeland. Newspaper descriptions of the scene prompted Bishop James Cannon, Jr. of Richmond, Virginia, to write a letter to the *Richmond Times Dispatch*. "The press reported that the ship came close enough to Miami for the refugees to see the lights of the city. The press also reported that the U.S. Coast Guard, under orders from Washington, followed the ship . . . . to prevent any people from landing on our shores. And during the days when this horrible tragedy was being enacted right at our doors, our government in Washington made no effort to relieve the desperate situation of these people, but on the contrary, gave orders that they be kept out of the country. Why did not the President, Secretary of State, Secretary of the Treasury, Secretary of Labor and other officials confer together to arrange for the landing of these refugees who had been brought in this maelstrom of distress and agony through no fault of their own? The failure to take any steps whatever to assist these distressed, persecuted Jews in their hour of extremity was one of the most disgraceful things which has happened in American history and leaves a stain and brand of shame upon the record of our nation."

Although the *The New York Times* did suggest that "the cruise of the *St. Louis* cries to high heaven of man's inhumanity to man," nowhere in the *Times* editorial, nor in the archives of the U.S. Government, is there a suggestion that the refugees be temporarily sheltered within the boundaries of the U.S. And nowhere was it communicated to the American public the fact that the passengers of the *St. Louis* were going to certain doom. It appears that none of the many papers that covered the *Saint Louis* managed to convey to their readers the desperate situation facing the passengers . . .

CHAPTER 7

A NICE LIFE

Editor's Note: After Peter's return from his Frankfurt-Berlin trip, he became increasingly frustrated by his lawyers' lack of response to his inquiries about the progress of his claims. Following are excerpts of his correspondence to them, leading to his replacing WM with a new lawyer.

FAX TO: HJ and WM
RECHTSANWALT UND NOTAR
9/19/91

Dear HJ:

I was about to follow your advice (letter 5/6/91) and write my uncle Rudolf Goldmann's (RG) children when I realized that I do not have any information about them, their names or how many they are. I also do not know anything about the so-called will of Alfons Goldmann (AG). I think it may be premature and possibly counter-productive to write them before I have more information.

I assume that RG'S children have already put through their claim for the estate of AG. I would like to have a copy of their claim as well as of the said will of AG.

Re: My claim for my share of the property of Alfons Goldmann's property at 18 Muhlstrasse Rosswein

I do not intend to request, nor will I accept, compensation from the German government in lieu of my share in the estate of AG. It is my wish to repossess the property, and establish my residence in it. I will, of course, compensate RG'S children for their share.

The fact that what brings us together is a dispute about our grandfather's will, turns what would be a most challenging occasion, mined with painful memories, into an unnatural and distasteful undertaking. I admit it does not bode well for the prospects of a dialogue, but I assure you that I will do whatever I can in good conscience to discuss with them the division of the property.

I intend to propose to the children of RG an agreement along the following lines: That the children of Rudolf Goldmann and the son of Dorothea Goldman (Peter Paz) agree in principle to bypass and disregard the said will of Alfons Goldmann in favor of a mutually arrived-at agreement for the division of AG's property; and that we also agree that the claim of RG's children is restricted to the property as described in the said will of AG and that they agree not to make any additional claims or demands against AG's property, the German Government or myself other then what will be provided for in our agreement.

A) That we agree that the estate of Alfons Goldmann at 18 Muhlstrasse be divided in to two equal parts. One part to go to the children of RG, the other part to go to me.
B) We agree to take joint action aimed at repossessing the estate of AG from the German Government.
C) We agree to share equally in the legal cost associated with this undertaking.
D) We agree that the son of Dorothea Goldmann will take possession of the repossessed property and take title to it.
E) We agree that the son of Dorothea Goldmann, Peter Paz, will compensate the children of Rudolf Goldmann for their part in the property at the prevailing market value of the property at the time and within a reasonable time period after receiving the deed.

I have given the issue considerable thought and have come to the following conclusions: I firmly believe that in consideration to all parties involved, both the living and the dead, the estate of Alfons Goldmann should be disposed of fairly and with a sense of justice. For after all is said and done it will be the final act of the legacies of Alfons, Rudolf, Dorthea and Magdalena Goldmann.

Since Rudolf Goldmann chose not to have contact with me, I have had no contact with his children. I, therefore, suggest that you convey this information to the children of R. Goldman.

Sincerely,
Peter Paz

FAX TO: HJ
RECHTSANWALT UND NOTAR
1/9/91

Dear HJ:

I am concerned about my application for German citizenship. Since I have not heard from you since my last inquiry I assume that everything is in order and it is just a question of time. However, I do not recall having filed an application. Please let me know, as soon as possible, what forms or documents, if any, you require in order to complete the process.

I am concerned about it since I am here already more then six months and sooner or later the French authorities will be asking me a lot of questions. I have been approached by a number of European companies for possible video and photography projects. However, without proper papers I am afraid that my ability to work in Europe will be extremely limited.

Regarding the Rosswein property, I would very much appreciate if you would let me know *what options are available to me before a final claim for the property is filed.*

I understand that you may be reluctant to write in English, and that you do not have a translator in your office. I will be happy to receive your reply in German. I thank you in advance for your consideration.

Yours sincerely,
Peter Paz

FAX TO: HJ
RECHTSANWALT UND NOTAR
8/6/91

Dear HJ:

If I understand correctly your May 6, 1991 letter you advise that
I should make the application to reclaim my German citizenship
at the German Consulate in Nice.

I have been away for the last three months. I plan to contact
the German consul next week. But as I do not have any of the
documents on the list (1-9) I am afraid, I will certainly get nowhere
in Nice.

In the spring of 1990 I set out to reclaim my German
citizenship. I contacted the German Consulate in New York.
Through an opening in the bullet-proof plexiglass, a young man
in his late twenties told me that, to the best of his knowledge,
I am neither a German nor do I have a right to claim German
citizenship. I am sure you can imagine my surprise. In fact, I was
so surprised that I decided to get in touch with some of my old
friends at *The New York Times* with the idea of doing an article about
the subject. Two weeks later I called the Consulate, requesting an
official interview with their legal attaché for the purpose of doing
a story about the rights of former Jewish Germans to reclaim
their citizenship and/or resettle in Germany. The "legal attaché"
I interviewed was the same young man I had spoken to through
the hole in the glass two weeks earlier. The taped interview is even
more astonishing than was the encounter through the hole in the
glass. I did not complete the story because I got overwhelmed with
our move to Europe.

The reason I asked you to help me in reclaiming my German
citizenship was that I was hoping to spare myself a long and
emotionally bruising fight. I understand that it might be a
time-consuming and costly undertaking for which I expected to
be billed.

I thank you in advance for your consideration.

Yours sincerely,
Peter Paz

FAX TO: HJ AND WM
RECHTSANWALT UND NOTAR
11/25/91

Dear HJ:

I am very frustrated that I have not received any response from you regarding my communications to you concerning the two matters the firm is handling for me: (1) my claim for Alfons Goldmann's (AG) property in Rosswein and (2) my claim for German citizenship.

It was MW's suggestion (letter 5/6/91) that I contact Rudolph Goldmann's (RG) children, with the idea of joining their claim for AG's property in Rosswein. In response I sent you a six-page fax on 9/5/91. In that fax I out-lined both my feeling about and the terms under which I might join such a claim. To date I have not received a response.

I see no reason why HJ should not continue to represent my effort to reclaim German citizenship provided that it is understood that *the resolution of this matter is Urgent and of the HIGHEST PRIORITY FOR ME . . . .*

For your record:

On April 5, 1991, telephone call to HJ:
I called you to enquire about my claim for AG's property. I was told that a claim on my behalf had been filed.

On April 5, 1991, Fax :
Telling you that although I was gratified to hear that a claim for AG's property in Rosswein was filed on my behalf, I was concerned at a remark you made during my telephone inquiry. You said that as far as you knew, my part of this property is a very small one.

1)   What is my part in this property?
2)   What is the document or documents that prompted you to make that statement? I have received no reply.

September 12, 1991, telephone to WM:

I called from Frankfurt asking for a meeting regarding HJ's proposed idea of a joint claim with RG's children.

September 13, 1991, meeting with WM:

I came to Berlin to discuss the joint claim idea with you and with HJ. I ended up discussing it with you. It was during that meeting, that for the first time, I was told that your firm is representing RG's children's claim for AG's property.

During that meeting, while leafing through the file looking for RG's will, you found an affidavit of sorts that indicated that, although AG left his property to both his son and his daughter, RG in his will left the entire property to his children, Miriam and John. And you said, "it was clearly not his to give."

I told you that I thought that if I was to join RG's children's claim, the most sensible way to resolve our differences would be to set up a meeting in Berlin with RG's children. I thought you had agreed. At the end of that meeting, I asked you if HJ would accept to undertake to represent my re-claming German citizenship with the understanding that I would pay all fees and expenses. HJ accepted and I signed a form of Power of Attorney.

On October 15, 1991, Fax:

I asked if there had been developments regarding the joint claim, and my reclaiming German citizenship.

I received no reply.

On October 24, 1991, Fax:

I re-sent the 9/15/91 Fax. I received no reply.

On October 24, telephone:

I called your office and I asked to speak to you. Your secretary said, "He is out" and hung-up on me.

On October 25, telephone:

I called your office again. Your secretary again said, "He is out," and again hung up on me.

On October 28, Fax to HJ:

I sent you an Urgent Fax in which I informed you of my calls and that your secretary had hung up on me, twice. Joining RG's children's claim for AG's property in Rosswein **is out of the question unless** I *have a commitment that I will get a prompt response to all telephone calls and my faxes will be answered within a timely fashion.*

In my fax, I asked you to please call me tomorrow afternoon (10/29/1991 between 17:00 and 21:00. *You may call me collect.*

In addition I asked for the following.

1. A copy of Alfons Goldmann's will.
2. A copy of RG's children's claim for Alfons Goldmann's property in Rosswein.
3. A copy of the claim for Alfons Goldmann's property you have filed on my behalf.
4. A copy of the application for German citizenship, if it has been filed.

As of 11/7/1991 I have received no response or acknowledgment of any of these communications.

In light of the above I have no choice but to conclude that your firm is no longer interested in the idea of a joint claim for Alfons Goldmann's property in Rosswein.

I will, therefore, be coming to Berlin within the next two weeks to engage other representation for my claim for Alfons Goldmann's property. I would be most grateful if you would send me a copy of the claim you have filed on my behalf for Alfons Goldmann's property.

Sincerely,
Peter Paz

Nice, February 1991

Dear Joe:

I have just come back from Berlin where I fired WM and HJ and took on a new lawyer, DB. An Israeli yuppie, with a German streak. In a cold, authoritative, flat tone he told me, "You are not going to get the house or anything close to its value." He went on to explain that Germany has a property law still in effect that says all contracts from 1933 to 1945 are illegal. Most Jewish claims for recovering property in Germany are based on that law. However, Germany has resisted applying this law to East Germany, and, he said, "My connections in the Bundestag are telling me that they are about to pass legislation that will exclude the former East Germany from that law . . . ."

FAX TO: DB
Berlin

February 25, 1991

Dear Mr. DB:

Thank you for taking the time to see me and telling me the facts as you know them. I was, however, profoundly shaken at the revelation of how the German Parliament intends to dispose of the problem of Jewish claims.

The thought that I might not get the Rosswein house, or even a reasonable compensation for it, was upsetting. But what has really shaken me is the realization that Germany, apparently, is once again engaged in fashioning a separate code of justice for Jews. Jews in Germany, it seems, are again about to be excluded from the protections provided to all Germans under the German Constitution. I trust that you will understand that as a survivor I cannot resign myself to accept this without a fight.

For the moment I would like you to take possession of the file from HJ. I did not go to see him following our meeting for the reason that I had been asking for a copy of that claim since the beginning of September 1991 (see my fax 11/8/91). HJ's pattern of not responding to any of my communications represents more than a culture gap. I have already notified him of my determination to seek other representation before our meeting.

I am enclosing a signed form of Power of Attorney and will instruct my bank in Frankfurt to transfer DM. 1000,00 to your account upon receiving your account number.

At this point in time, I would like to suggest that you take steps to obtain the copy of the claim for Alfons Goldmann's house in Rosswein that HJ filed on my behalf, as well as all documents and other material in HJ's possession.

Before I go to the German Consulate in Marseille to reclaim my German citizenship, I would be grateful if you could check again whether my application for German citizenship can be done through your office. I am attaching a related document that HJ sent me. *It contains a list of required documents of which I have none. I believe, however, that the documents are in the file that HJ will hopefully transfer to you.*

I thank you again.

Sincerely,
Peter Paz

Nice, December 1991

Dear Lyrissa:

How does it feel being at college away from home, having no one telling you what to do, pushing you around? I hope you enjoy it, savor it, and make the most of it while it lasts. I think your choice of subjects is a good one. Do not be surprised if things seem not to work out perfectly at the beginning, it's normal. I was a total wreck before my first photo assignments (always managed to forget something), but in school it was different. It was the place to make mistakes, one teacher used to remind me. She wasn't too popular, but I still think she was the best. She taught literature and was a freak about doing your best. Let others worry about perfection.

Your mom said that you have no phone in your room. With the ten hours time difference it is going to make it more difficult to call you, but I do hope you won't worry about it too much. I love you and think of you, even though I take forever to write. (Julie didn't have a phone in her room either and she went to Yale, a fat Ivy League college, neither did Marc-Andrew,[*] no one did. Don't make a big thing of it).

As to your question of why getting fired from the job I had after I quit dancing was the best thing that ever happened to me: of course, I was unhappy being fired at the time. But the fact that it was not my fault was what made me think of going on my own. It almost forced me to take a gamble on myself. I would never have traveled around the world as I have had I not been fired from that job. I was lucky. So I was lucky, even though it seemed difficult at the time. Starting out as a photographer was amazingly uncomplicated then, compared to what it is like today. There were fewer photographers, there were no automatic cameras of any kind, no computers that could pick up parts of different photographs and combine them into a new picture.

True, I knew no one, had no portfolio, no contacts of any kind. What I did have was old fashioned chutzpah, an old Russian camera, and a vague feeling that I could do it. The biggest obstacle

---

[*]   Beverly's son

was convincing someone else to believe it. But it was a time when art directors actually spoke to anyone who called. And they took the time to see me and look at my work. It is different today. If things then were as difficult as they are today, I would certainly have taken a "proper job," I would be crazy not to.

I enclose a story "'Krista's Party," it's about my friend Aaron. We used to visit him in Long Island. Swim in his pool. His daughter, Jordana, is about your age. Aaron has a very proper job, making tons of money. "I know I kidded you all this time about your leaving New York," he said over lunch, just before we left for France, "I thought you would never do it. But now that you're going, I'll tell you the truth: I was jealous. I wish I could do it."

He had what in New York is called "a big job" with a big salary and a big bonus and an office with two windows facing Park Avenue. When he discovered one morning that his office had been moved, he thought, "They no longer appreciate me as they did before. Should I look for a new job? What if we have to move? And what if they take my one remaining window away?" Having a proper job is great for some people, but then there is always the possibility that one day that job may no longer be there.

I hope we can see each other in the spring.

Much love,
Dad

KRISTA'S PARTY

"The thing about pickled herring," Y. L. Peretz wrote, "is that the longer it stays in the brine, the more pickled it gets. The more pickled it gets the less it tastes like herring. So one must be forever careful not to leave it too long, or God forbid, forget it in the brine."

Over the holidays, Beverly and I were invited to cake and coffee by Krista, a decorator and friend. Her apartment was, of course, still undecorated, so we ended up at her husband's office. Jean Michel, a Frenchman from Alsace, late forty to fiftyish, has eight windows in his office, that is, 4+4 windows. He is a big wheel in France Telecom, but *eight* windows?

As I shook his hand, his wife's strudel stuck in my throat. "Are you feeling OK?" he asked. "I am all right, it's just that I never knew anyone with eight windows," I said. To make sure I saw right, I kept counting the windows.

It was clear he did not understand my amazement. So I told him about my friend Aaron in New York, who had two windows facing Park Avenue. Jean Michel was duly impressed. But when I told him that I was going to write my friend to tell him that I met someone who actually has *eight* windows—that is, 4+4 windows—facing the Matisse-blue sea, he started laughing. Then I told him how Aaron one morning discovered his office had been moved overnight, to a space with only one window—no laughing matter. I tried to explain: "My friend's world," I said, had actually shrunk! Overnight." For a moment, he looked at me straight in the eye, then seeing that I was serious, he burst out laughing so hard his wife's strudel got stuck in *his* throat. He turned red and began shedding tears.

Being German, I thought, Alsatian or whatever, he didn't understand my New York friend's one window or two-windows dilemma. So in my best French, and with a straight face, I went on trying to explain why for my friend the loss of a window was such a blow. "He was afraid," I said. "that they would ask him to head the Dallas office. That is, move to Dallas."

"Dallas?" he said, in a heavy French accent, "What's wrong with Dallas?" still shaking with laughter, "Wonderful town, nice people!"

"On TV," I said, and went on to explain that my friend's wife, on hearing about the loss of his window, announced: "If you are going to Dallas, I am not going with you."

That set Jean Michel roaring with laughter once more. "I would go to Dallas," he said, choking again on his mouthful. Worried that it would do him in, or that it would end up on me, I gave up trying to explain. When he was reasonably calm I asked him if I could come back sometime to take a photograph of him with his eight windows. He looked at me strangely, like "Are you putting me on?" "Without a photo," I said as fast as I could, "my friend in New York will never believe it." His face was blank. "He is a lawyer," I added just to make sure he understood. At which point, Jean Michel started laughing all over again, a wild thigh-slapping contagious laughter, bursting out with pieces of nuts and raisins all over the place.

"He will never understand what it means to lose a window," I realized. I gave up, letting myself go, swept away by his laughter.

Nice, September 1992

Dear Joe:

I read Appelfeld's book* in the glow of your visit. As he takes out the feathers of the pillow that is Badenheim, Appelfeld leaves his ghost-like characters stranded. A cloud hangs over the town, casting a shadow over their summer vacation. Hope is slowly eclipsed by acceptance, as despair looks in from the windows and creeps in under the door at night. Gradually, almost imperceptibly they wake up to a world where one must take a sliver of light from a cold autumn moon, reflected on a tree's last leaf, as a sign of spring or perish. It was impossible to read *Badenheim 1939* without feeling oppressed by the knowledge that the Badenheims have become a disagreeable, but an acceptable part of our landscape.

I started another month of immersion in French last week. Doing eight hours of French a day was just what I needed for a much-needed improvement in French, and to see where this writing was going.

Hoping to engage my class in discussion, I prepared myself to talk about the refugee problem in France and Germany, in French. I wrote detailed notes and a list of questions. But as I opened the morning paper I saw an image of six photographers falling over themselves to take a picture of Bill Clinton's cat. On the facing page was a Reuter's dispatch from London to the effect that Prime Minister John Major was attacked for blocking a British charity organization from taking in Bosnians, mostly women and children, stranded on the Austrian border. His spokesman announced that Great Britain may allow entry to six of them, and that three more are under consideration.

Facing these pages, before my mind was entirely awake, properly anchored, sent it wandering back to Vienna, where in 1935, Edmund Husserl, in a series of lectures, warned that

---

* *Badenheim 1939 by* Ahron Appelfeld is the story of Jewish vacationers in a town near Vienna in the spring of 1939. The vacationers are so intent on clinging to their way of life that they delude themselves as to the purpose of the German occupation of the town until it is too late, and all the Jews are deported.

European civilization was in a crisis. The crisis he spoke of seemed to him so profound that he suggested that European civilization might not survive it.

I could not help but wonder, "Did European civilization survive?" So I decided to ask my class.

In my class of six this month were: a Norwegian my age from Oslo, owner of a supermarket; a Spanish beauty of 22, exporting movie trailers, she was here the month before, will be staying the next, and then will go on to Berlin for three months of intensive German; a young, shy Viennese girl who thought Vienna just a beautiful postcard city, "But there is somesing missing, I don't know what," she kept saying; a young German in his twenties, exporting his family's steel (what else?); a young Iranian whose family had climbed aboard its rugs and flown out to Frankfurt just before the unsmiling Ayatollah landed in Tehran. Two middle-aged American woman lawyers, divorced. The one from Denver Colorado, plain as a carrot, suggested that it was a man's world where women had been unwitting passengers as men drove mankind into a ditch. Her friend was a Jewish liberal public policy lawyer from Memphis, Tennessee, formerly from New York. And a young eccentric German veterinarian doctor who drove non stop from Hamburg to Villefranche and was so fatigued on arrival that he lay down Friday afternoon and woke up Tuesday morning, missing the first day of school. "Somesing woke me up," he said, very slowly, negotiating his words like a sleepwalker. "I looked at my watch, it was close to midnight. I did not want to put the light on and so I reached into my drug bag, took a pill and went back to sleep."

"From Friday to Tuesday?" said Christian, our teacher, a short Corsican with more mischief then surprise.

"Well," said Rudolf, rubbing his fingers over his lips, choosing his words carefully, "I must have taken the wrong pill."

"What do you mean?" asked Christian, with naked mischief.

"I have those pills for horses," Rudolf said, as if talking to himself. "I must have taken one of them."

"I can't hear you," Christian kept after him.

"I took the wrong pill," whispered Rudolf to his fingers.

Eric, the Oslo supermarket owner was the only one uncomfortable with my question. "It is unfair of you to lay this on us," he said. "Inga and I give what we can at our church; there is no solution to this problem. Why should we take the women and children of Sarajevo and not the women and children of Somalia?"

"So it all comes down to shelf space, like your supermarket," I said. "It does, in a way," Eric conceded reluctantly.

"If we accept more refugees, we will be helping our Nazis," said the young German, which was Roosevelt's line in 1939. The first-generation German from Iran agreed.

"What about you, Rudolf?" asked Christian.

He was taking his time, still rubbing his fingers over his lips, from left to right, left to right, "I . . . . agree . . . . with . . . . Eric," he said. "It is all about shelf space."

"But Peter said that," said Eric.

"I . . . know . . . but it is . . . your fault."

"What do you mean!" retorted Eric, sitting up in surprise.

"If the manager of a supermarket orders more products then he has shelf space for then everysing is a mess."

"You should say this to your Chancellor, Mr. Kohl."

"Ya, I do! I am with the Greens, but he does not listen."

"What kind of world do you think we would we be living in today," asked the lawyer from Memphis over lunch, "if John Major, Herman Kohl and George Bush were in power then instead of Churchill, Roosevelt, Hitler and Stalin?" "Between you and me," I said, "I have a sneaking suspicion that we are living in it, but of course I won't admit it even to myself."

Again I ask your indulgence for yet another somber note from the city of sunshine where neither *Badenheim* nor *Heimat* cast a shadow.

My love to Mildred and the group.

Love,
Peter

THE HOLOCAUST AS POLITICS

Nice, December 1991

When Alex and his wife, both Holocaust survivors came for tea with Tanya, their twenty-four-year-old daughter, the subject of *Heimat* came up. We had been watching it on TV for weeks, a portrait of a German family from the last days of the Weimar Republic to the height of the Cold War.

"In sixteen hours of film, there is just one sentence that obliquely refers to the extermination of Jews, it's unbelievable!" said Alex.

"You want the filmmaker to condemn them," I said.

"I like a spade to be called a spade," said Alex. Beverly agreed.

"If you did, then we would have Hollywood," I said, where acts of evil are committed by people who are monsters. *Heimat* is a portrait of life, of banality, its characters look like me, like you, like our friends, living their lives as loyal citizens, responsible members of the community, trying to keep their heads above water. *Heimat* is a state of mind. It is universal. All it takes to become a citizen of *Heimat* is to go along, do nothing, go on with life, adjust, learn to live with it, or pretend, if one can, that what one suspects, does not in fact take place. That's what the film tells me. And that's what I suspect life was like everywhere, just like in Badenheim, that's why it disturbs me so."

"Looking at *Heimat*, future generations will get the wrong message about the Final Solution," said Julie, a feminist out of Yale, in the Femis Film School in Paris.

"Or they may even believe there was no final solution," I said.

"Exactly!" she said. "The filmmaker has a responsibility to society. As such, *Heimet* fails!"

"Then we are back to *The Triumph of the Will* and *The Battleship Potemkin,* with the Leni Riefenstahls and Sergei Eisensteins, serving society, or some other march, saving its kind from the rest of mankind; we're back in Badenheim, if you will."

"Not as inmates," she said.

"Just the same," I said. At which point the doorbell rang. There followed an awkward silence when Krista and her German friend walked in . . .

*   *   *

It is next to impossible not to notice the Holocaust these days. It is getting more popular every day. People are falling over themselves trying to get monuments, memorial centers, and museums erected in their communities. Poles, Croats, Rumanians, Slovaks, and Germans tripped over each other to get invited to the ceremony commemorating the uprising of the ghetto of Warsaw. It was quite a show in Warsaw.

Here in France, one of the national TV channels had its entire evening dedicated to the subject. Two films, made in Israel by Israelis, were shown, followed by discussions. Although focusing on the story of the uprising, the films seemed to digress, telling much of the story of Hitler's war against the Jews instead. So much so that I began to wonder why. I disliked both films equally and was upset as I watched them. The films were more like tailored high-school teaching materials than films documenting history. Their unsubtle attempt to highlight the Zionist credentials of the uprising's organizers reminded me of the films of the Russian Revolution that we watched every Tuesday night on the dining room wall, forty years earlier, in the Kibbutz by the Sea. There was propaganda in those films—simple, old-fashioned propaganda.

But in these films, it was a question of rewriting history. Archival footage from the Warsaw uprising was being used to tell the story of the Holocaust. At the end, a young woman historian bristled when an equally young interviewer asked if the ethnic cleansing going on in ex-Yugoslavia did not evoke the Holocaust. "The Jews of Europe were murdered because they were Jewish, not Zionists," she said.

So why had the filmmakers gone out of their way to stress the credentials of the few Zionists involved? Here it was not a question of rooting, it was a question of rewriting history. The Jews of Europe were murdered because they were Jewish, not Zionists. And why were the filmmakers, fifty years later retelling the story of the Holocaust as a footnote to the uprising of the Warsaw Ghetto?

"I think they were just trying to put the uprising in the context of history," ventured Beverly. "So it seems," I replied, "but the trouble is, most Americans, having sat out the Holocaust, dare not raise questions. They take everything they see here as an article of faith."

But I was upset about the films and took personally the question of heroic circumstances. What started out as the Grand March to a Jewish homeland has become the Grand March from Holocaust to the redemption of Greater Israel. Can they not let the dead of the Holocaust—all six million—rest in peace?

On the other hand, Jewish nationalism can no longer do without the Holocaust. Amos Elon recounts a conversation between Richard Crossman, a British Labor politician, and a retired Israeli diplomat. Crossman, a longtime friend of Israel, was complaining bitterly about Israel's intransigence concerning Palestinians rights, and especially that of the then Prime Minister Golda Meir. The diplomat sadly nodded his assent. Then he tried to make Golda Meir's intransigence comprehensible to Crossman by invoking the memory of the Holocaust. "We are a traumatized people," he said. "Please understand!" "Certainly," Crossman responded. "You certainly are a traumatized people! But you are a traumatized people with an atom bomb! Such people belong behind bars!" That conversation took place in 1972. As Ahron Appelfeld in *Badenheim 1939* put it recently: "For us the Holocaust is like looking into the sun."

Israel, 1955

In our last year of high school, our class went on a field trip to a neighboring kibbutz founded by survivors of the Warsaw Ghetto. We walked by mural-size photographs and reproductions of some documents. And that was the chapter of the Holocaust. There was no discussion, no one asked questions.

Since the extreme right has come to power, Holocaust studies in the classroom are supplemented by government-subsidized school tours to Poland. Thousands of high school students take part in these tours—called Marches of the Living—accompanied by former concentration camp inmates who act as special guides. The students usually fly first to Warsaw and visit the former ghetto. From there, they continue to Treblinka and Auschwitz, which is the high point. Singing Israeli songs, waving Israeli national flags, tee shirts emblazoned with a big Star of David and the inscription "Israel or Israel LIVES," the young visitors march through the Auschwitz *Stammlager* guided by a former inmate. At nearby Birkenau, they hoist their flags at the former crematoria and intone a special prayer for the safety of soldiers in the Israeli Army, wherever they may be.

Upon their return from Poland, some of the young participants told the press that on the site of the former extermination camp they had become "better Zionists." They had become convinced that Israel must keep every square centimeter of Eretz Israel, territorial compromise was impossible. According to one of the guidebooks published by the Ministry of Education for these trips, Auschwitz exemplified the world's immutable hatred for Jews, a hatred which has always existed and will always exist as long as there are gentiles and Jews. Another text decries both current Polish anti-Semitism and the fact that the Polish government recognizes the Palestinians' right to self-determination—as if they were the same thing.

Which brings me back to the question of: "What is left of my story that is worth telling? What is left is the story of how my story became a joke. Or the story of how a former resident of Badenheim woke up one day to find himself living in Heimat."

France, 1993

In October, Leni Riefenstahl, now ninety-three years old, was on the French-German channel Arte. She was diving thirty meters deep, shooting fish and the underwater landscape in the Pacific that looked astonishingly like the images of the Alps she shot sixty years earlier for her film *The Holy Mountain*.

For three hours, her films were intercut with an interview covering her life and her work. "I am an artist," she said when allusions were repeatedly made, suggesting that her films advanced the Nazi cause.

"You worked with Marlene Dietrich. What was she like?" she was asked.

"She was beautiful, seductive, melancholy. She got all the good parts. I, on the other hand, got the roles of women struggling for ideals against those instincts."

"Why did you not leave Germany like Marlene Dietrich did?"

"It is my Heimat. I was free here, I could not see myself living as a foreigner anywhere."

"Do you feel that your films may have helped the Nazi cause?"

"I am an artist, I did not understand politics. It did not interest me, then or now. I was never a party member. I never knew what they were doing. As far as I knew, Hitler was saving Germany. That's what eighty percent of the Germans thought, and many in England and America did as well. When I saw the films from Buchenwald, I was horrified. There were only two ways left, I thought: "To die, or live with the guilt and the shame forever.""

Past collaboration with Germany is still haunting France, from the man on the street to the man in the Elysée Palace. For those who were hoping that the trail of Maurice Papon* would lead to a national cleansing, bearing witness to what happened to the Jews of France, acknowledging the victims and the survivors, it has become a great disappointment. I wonder how much

---

* Maurice Papon, a French official in the pro-Nazi Vichy government, was accused of signing deportation orders for 1,600 French Jews, many of them children, who were sent to Auschwitz where few survived. He was found not guilty of

of it is a reflection of the general sentiment, expressed with reservation by the French, that the Jewish state has become a "fascist state." After all, why should they be searching their conscience when they see the Jewish state behaving as it does?

Conference on Exclusion, 1993

A conference on Nationalism and Exclusion was held in Nice last month. Billed as a dialogue between Palestinians and Israelis, it started with everyone walking through metal detectors. The PLO, though invited, did not show up, protesting the recent deportation of the 415 Palestinians to Lebanon.

Schlomo Albez began by stating that peace is in the overriding interest of both Israel and the Palestinians. Yael Dayan opened her remarks by complaining that she had the most uncomfortable chair and that her knees were up against two table ends. The UN Commissioner of Refugees, an Arab, offered her his chair, but not his place. She accepted and went on to say, "If I could go to Tunis to see Arafat, I don't see why he couldn't come to Nice." She closed her remarks with a promise and warning, "Although we possess a great arsenal, we feel threatened. To those on the other side who believe that there is a military solution to the conflict, I will say that we will not be a party to an agreement that will leave us feeling threatened."

Nice has a large Jewish as well as Arab population. Many were there, waiting to engage the panel. But even before the microphone was let loose, a Lebanese member of the panel brought up the deportation. "The deportation was a political mistake," conceded Mr. Adler, a local political analyst, after being pressed. There followed fifteen minutes of bitter characterizations and denunciations. I never did get a chance to ask Mr. Adler, a lawyer, why he chose the term "political mistake." So I went up to the podium and asked him after the panel had concluded.

"I called it a political mistake because that's what it was," he said.

---

their murders. After a six-month trial, he was sentenced to ten years in prison in 1998 for crimes against humanity. In 2002, he was freed on grounds of ill health. The French were divided on the usefulness of the trial, questioning the validity of trying war criminals so long after the end of the war, which reopened the painful examination of the Vichy government's role in collaboration with Germany.

"Was it not a violation of international law?" I asked.

"It was not," he said.

"Then neither was the deportation of my family and myself in 1943," I said. He got red in the face, turned and walked away.

Schlomo Albez was at the other end of the podium. I walked over and asked him about Mr. Adler's remarks. "Is he one of your guys?" I asked. "No, he speaks for himself." "So, what do you think?" I asked.

"It was a political mistake," he said. "A terrible mistake, I was in the room when the news came. There was panic—we had to do something fast, but nobody thinks it was not a mistake."

"Was it not a violation of international law?"

"Look," he said, containing his anger. "We have enough of our own liberal do-gooders. We don't need you!"

"The reason I brought it up," I said, "is that hearing Mr. Adler say it with so much conviction, I began to wonder whether the phrase "political mistake" is for public consumption or is it a case of a government believing its own propaganda?"

"I know what you are saying. You are right, but what else can we say," he shrugged his reply.

For me, the deportation episode has all the ingredients of a Sholem Aleichem's story from Chelm. "Israel cannot afford to appear weak," said his government spokesman before Mr. Rabin ordered the deportations, hoping to cut the ground out from under Hamas. As it turned out, Hamas dragged Rabin's government, the high court, the Jewish state, and every Jew, I dare say, with them into a no-man's-land, as the world watched. It makes me think that there may be a God after all. This is his kind of a joke. He is laughing at us, his "Chosen." A rolling, thunderous, Falstaffian laugh. I never before understood the saying "Man thinks God laughs." If this isn't it, what could it be? Seeing us, after two thousand years of living in banishment, building Badenheims in the Promised Land, what else could God do but laugh?

It is not that I am not aware of the difference between Israel's deportation of 415 Palestinians and my own deportation. But since governments in Jerusalem started telling the world how different their actions are, I have begun to look at the similarities.

Kibbutz Afek, October 1946

Three months after Gilli ended up being shot dead by mistake, along with the dogs belonging to the Palestinian shepherds, the King David Hotel in Jerusalem was bombed by Menachem Begin's Irgun.* The explosion killed eighty-two people, including forty Palestinians and seventeen Jews. The British responded by hanging three suspected Irgun terrorists. Begin retaliated by ordering the execution of two British sergeants held captive by the Irgun. Their bodies were booby-trapped and left hanging upside down.

On the night of April 9, 1948, Yair Stern's gang massacred every man, woman, child, and dog of Dier Yasin, setting off the flight of over 600,000 Palestinian Arabs from what was designated Israeli territory under the UN partition of 1947. At the time, Begin's men were called a gang of terrorists and neo-Fascists. But no charges of crime or misconduct were ever filed against anyone involved.

Awarding the Nobel Peace Prize to Menachem Begin must have played a part in his decision to reject General Sharon request to launch a nuclear strike against Syria. But on his watch, Christian Phalangist's entered Sabra and Shatilah to massacre 800-2,000 Palestinian men, women, and children. Sharon was now a member of the Cabinet and a folk hero, "King of Israel."

---

* Irgun, shorthand for Irgun Tsvai Leumi . . . Hebrew for "National Military Organization", was a paramilitary Zionist group that operated in the British Mandate of Palestine from 1931 to 1948 . . . It was classified by British authorities as a "terrorist organization" but many Jews considered it to be a "liberation movement." Its political association with Revisionist Zionism rendered it a predecessor movement to modern Israel's "right-wing" Likud party/coalition.

LETTERS

Nice, France, 1993

Dear Lyrissa:

One day, when you were five, when I was driving you to school, you asked me "Why do I have only one grandmother and grandfather?" I had often thought about your question, a simple question. "My family died in the war, "I said. I did not have a better answer because I could never bring myself to think about it. Now, in the faraway silence of sunny blue Nice, I hear the echo of your question and I still have no better answer. But the other day, out of a blue envelope, fell Cousin Miriam.

I could not find either a cousin or a Miriam in my memory. But you know about my memory. As I opened the envelope a photograph fell out, a family picture—a man, a woman, two children, and a dog. No one I had ever seen, and on the back of the photo, in pencil, was written: John, Zoey, David and Miriam, 1992. Apparently Uncle Rudolf, my mother's brother, of whom, Grandmother once had written, "He does not give me money for stamps," had a daughter. My Cousin Miriam.

I started reading. My lawyer in Berlin, HJ, gave me your address," said the note. "I was going to call you as soon as HJ gave me your address. But I was afraid that I would be overcome with emotions. I have been looking for you, in Israel and America, for more then twenty years. Now that I have found you, I know the family is whole." Signed, Your Cousin Miriam London, Menorah, West Australia.

I put the card down and looked once again at the picture, contemplating the idea of "family." Uncle Rudolf and the notion of a real family out there in the boondocks of West Australia, was doing crocodile circles in my head. Not having a family seems so natural. I really meant it when, after hearing stories about terrible parents in my therapy group, I told them I felt fortunate to be an orphan. But now, turning the card in my hand, there was something tantalizing, captivating in the idea of "family." "She looks like she could very well be the local president of Hadassa in Columbus,

Ohio or anywhere else," said Beverly, on seeing the picture. I said, "More like a Jewish nun." Beverly urged, "Give her a chance."

So I did. I wrote her a letter, with a photo of myself. A week or two later Beverly, too, wrote as well, inviting them to visit whenever they planned to come to Europe or go to Israel. (Miriam's brother and his family live in Revivim, a kibbutz in Israel.)

Love,
Dad

Nice, France, 1993

My dear Mugwump:

I read your letter over and over. It made me feel truly happy! You write well and I thank you for the photos, they are wonderful. I was actually in the process of writing you a whole other letter, about how Cousin Miriam did not write back, etc. Well guess what? She wrote—five months later, but she wrote, and that's what counts, letter enclosed. At the rate I write I should be the last one to complain, even quietly to myself. Of course, I feel bad about it. At times, I thought of writing, asking her to return the pictures I sent and consider what she called "a search for you" for what it was: a way to make herself feel good. But I decided not to. Before writing her I thought that the reason she wrote me was to make herself feel better. Not knowing where I was became a pebble in her shoe, so to speak. Now that she found me, life could go on as before, tranquility is restored. After all, her father, Uncle Rudolf, always knew where I was.

The problem with people like me who survived the war, and people like Uncle Rudolph, who got away before the sky fell down and witnessed its falling on us, is that they feel bad for getting out, leaving us behind. Uncle Rudolf must have felt so bad about it, and so angry at his dead sister, my mother and me, that he never wrote, could not bring himself to acknowledge that I existed, even by implication. "He won't even give me money for stamps," said my grandmother (his mother) in one of her last letters to me before she died.

And, of course, I felt bad, too—still do—having survived the sky falling. I kept wondering: why me? Surely I must have had something to do with it? But I heard this voice in me, whispering, "You are alive! What more can you ask for? What more is there?" I still hear it.

After the war ended those who squeaked through, like Uncle Rudolf (Cousin Miriam was still a baby) and those who read about it in the papers, wanted to forget, to put it behind them as soon as possible, and to "go on with life," which is understandable, natural. But there were many of us who survived. We became a living reminder to what they wished or imagined they could have done, but did not do, like the tailors, who felt so burdened by that feeling that they had to unburden themselves before me as we were standing at the door, shaking hands. They were the brave ones.

As I started writing these notes, it was only natural I would be a bit confused. Where do I start? Should I start at the beginning? But where is the beginning? Most of my life before Palestine was wiped out, disappeared, in a cloud . . . .

Nice, 1993

Dear Larry and Rochelle*,

A few notes in the sun and our doings in the city where nothing is happening, just in case you got the impression that I am lost or drowned in my musings.

There was a time when this city was dominated by Rome and the ancient blue sea. Today, one has only to look at the shops selling ribbons, earrings, necklaces, pearls, diamonds (false and real) rhinestone sweaters, T-shirts, booties, sunglasses and high-tech leashes to realize that this is a dog's world, and Nice must be their undisputed capital. The city, which officially has been broke ever since the last mayor ran away with the money, has just bought a fleet of Suzuki motorcycles equipped with a high-tech elephant's nose "dog-mobiles," that are supposed to pick up after them, that is if one has not stepped in it first.

The next most important thing that matters here is, of course, suntan. Shops selling products and salons devoted to a "safe and perfect suntan" are everywhere. Anyone who still thinks of a dog's world in the old-fashioned way should just look at the pictures in the paper. On days when there is no scandal, the front page of the *Nice Matin* has a perfectly tanned topless blond or brunette, or a dignified portrait of a poodle with perfectly sculptured hair that looks like the work of a master gardener. I myself can't resist thinking, what would Matisse's paintings look like were he to paint today?

Down here, they blame it all on Leon Blum, of course! Not because he was Jewish, but because he believed that every French man and women deserved a month-long vacation paid by the state. So when the Germans invaded France, the French promptly handed Mr. Blum over to the Germans, who, in turn, sent him to Auschwitz.

But, Leon Blum survived the war, as did the idea of the French vacation. So every year, on the last day of June, the French stuff their

---

* Friends Larry and Rochelle Sullivan. Rochelle had been in Peter's group therapy with therapists Joe Katz and Mildred Newman.

children, in-laws, dogs and themselves into tiny little paper-mâché cars and start the five hundred miles mad race to the Cote d'Azur. Those who make it (the French are definitely not among the world's most careful drivers), proceed to roast themselves in the sun with the same single-mindedness they did driving down here. After all, they have to have something to show for a thousand mile race and a month in the sun.

It is now the beginning of autumn here. The tourists, except for a few odd Englishmen are gone. In the Café Turin on our corner, J. C. normally arrives around lunchtime with his dog Max in a basket. (I call him J. C. for Jean Claude, a friend of ours who lost his shirt trying to convert the old New York's Old Headless Horseman Bar into a chic French restaurant by painting the place black, ceiling and all).

After putting the basket on the ground, J. C. draws a paper towel from his pocket and carefully wipes off the chair. He then pulls a pillow from the basket and places it on the chair, at which point Max jumps on the pillow and J. C. sits down and looks at the menu.

On most days, J. C. orders oysters, crabs, mussels and snails, etc. (all uncooked) and a bottle of rosé. Max, being a dog, slurps the oyster as soon as J. C. manages to place it on his plate. And then begins a daily scene in which J. C. tells Max, "Behave yourself, slow down, they'll think I don't feed you." But Max bangs his paw on the table, forcing J. C. to keep up, slurps his oysters as fast as Max does. To slow his dog down, J. C. pours a bit of Côte de Provence in Max's dish which Max slurps up at the speed of light, and bangs his paw on the table, demanding more. When it is slow in coming, Max gives J. C. the "come on, be a mensch" look, tilting his head sideways until J. C. breaks down and pours him more wine. And so it goes, except for the days when J. C. and Max come for breakfast. Then J. C. dunks his croissant in a "grand crème" and shares it with Max—one for me one for you—as he reads the *Nice Matin*.

Although a daily feature at the Café Turin, J. C. and his dog, I am told, have never made it to the front page of the *Nice Matin*. The possible reasons why a dog and his master, wearing identical T-shirts and lunching on oysters and snails, fails to be news in the local paper stumped me. Those I've asked either didn't know or won't tell. I am beginning to think that the French lack a sense of humor. Or perhaps J. C. and his dog are old Communists, who have never been popular in this part of France. I would not be surprised if the *Nice Matin*, a good old right-wing newspaper, takes the position of wait-and-see about Communism, before immortalizing J. C. and his dog.

We do not have a dog, yet. But in the spirit of things Niçois, Beverly and I took the train to Genoa and Portofino. Mostly to eat pasta, the kind of pasta only Italians in Italy make, and to celebrate our 56th birthdays. The youngest houses on Genoa's Via Garibaldi are five hundred years old. Banks, bakeries, bookshops, churches and the City Hall, all a living testimony to the Age of Reason, when man began to question God, himself and his place in the universe. Sarajevo was but a thousand miles away, too far for us to hear the sound of the cannon shells falling on the city. But as I looked at the cathedral-like Genoa mansions I could not help but wonder, "What is left of the spirit of Man that inspired those creations, now that Man has become Master of the Universe?"

We were back in Nice in time to toast Rabin and Arafat's historic hand—shake. It looks like it may be may the beginning of a relationship. If it is the return of reason and the end of a hundred years of the march of folly, I believe we can make it. For the moment I am hopeful, but as Santayana said: "One must always, without necessarily being a pessimist, be prepared for the worst." It may be just a pause, due to exhaustion of body and spirit, from whatever drives us in the name of survival, to self-destruct, and it will raise its head again, intoxicating us to take yet another run at the cliff.

On second thought, I think the real reason Max and J. C. haven't made it to the cover of the people's daily is that, unlike "them dogs" who show off their diamonds strolling along the Promenade des Anglais, Max wears a simple, rolled-up red handkerchief around his neck. Love and all the best, hope to see you soon. Peter

Nice, France, 1993

Dear Joe and Esther:

It seems so long since your last thoughtful letter, so long that I ask to be forgiven for my silence and for this long grim letter.

The daily savagery from Serbanica, Gaza, Soweto and Israel goes on. It is beamed back into our living room, in thirty-second clips at the end of the day. I notice my tolerance to the savagery rises as it becomes more gruesome. I am being vaccinated, one small dose of neatly packaged horror at a time. In time, indifference—the mind's (natural?) self-protective mechanism—will set in, I suppose, and I will be able to write a decent letter about life in the sun. For the moment, I savor my feeling of horror. It may be no more then a mute, empty gesture to resist, being swept away by the tide of resignation, acceptance, trying to hold on to myself.

Between wondering whether the situation is worse or better then it was then, I realize that, like beauty, savagery is in the eye of the beholder. I am sick with it, but I don't seem to be able to disengage. Desperate for a sign that there is some meaning to the madness, I stay tuned. Tuned to the spectacle of man's compulsive march to ruin.

Seeing how easy—almost naturally, we all shift into a state of acceptance—is a sobering sight. It should not have surprised me, but it does. Somehow it is impossible for me to accept that the first half of this century has left no lasting mark on our civilization, that we "the people of the book" have become part of it all. It defies comprehension.

The trouble is that instead of doing something useful, like writing, my mind wanders. Is the world really different from what it was like then? And other important questions plague me, like: What if the people then were exposed to the same sixty-second clips of horror at the end their day, before bedtime, would they have slept better than we do today? And perhaps the most important question of all: Can we still recognize savagery, or has it too become a mere abstraction?

We may not like it, but if one is to remain a productive member of society, one has to be able to disengage. Searching desperately for signs that there is some end to the madness, that something can be done to stop it, is dangerous and may in itself be madness. It certainly is unproductive.

So I stay tuned to the spectacle of man's compulsive march to wherever it is leading, and go to the beach. The sun is out, one of life's few remaining pleasures. The so-called popular music—the stuff that blasts you out of most restaurants used by our children's generation to give us the proverbial finger—is outlawed. And most important of all is facing the magic blues of Matisse and being surrounded by the earthly delights in the shape of, you guessed it, French tits. I would like to think that when he mixed his blues Matisse beheld at least one of those sublime twins of creation. To think that the heart has the power to lift us out of ourselves, and also to inspire what is savage in us.

But here, Sarajevo is but a train ride away, and the consciousness of being Jewish ever present. The idea of 'living well is the best revenge' has a hollow, sad ring to it, a bad joke. Perhaps one can still utter it in the suffocating heat of a summer drinking party or in the heat of a Southern backwater town, or in a New York townhouse.

Here I face the sea and myself and I feel shame, deep unrelenting shame at the indifference of a world in the face of savagery. Serbs, Croats and Israelis, civilians fighting in the name of nationalist agendas that defy human decency.

Being witness to the daily savagery as I sit in my comfortable living-room has given my journey a sense of urgency, but simplified it, too. It is a kind of Passover here. Every day I am reminded of where I come from and what it was like. I am also reminded that compromising with injustice, perpetrated by the State, leads to evil.

Love,
Peter

FAX TO: DB
December 1992

Dear DB:

When you called last December to say "Stop sending me messages,
I have nothing to say to you, I will get back to you after January
15. If you don't like it you can have your money back," I took you
at your word that you would get back to me after Jan. 15. Your
latest fax advising that you are out of town until Feb. 12 came as
a surprise to me.

Seen in the context of more then a year of inaction and your
silence in the face of half a dozen communications restating my
reasons for the urgency of the citizenship case, that fax raises
questions about whether you are prepared to honor your obligation
to this case.

Therefore, I have decided to take you up on your offer to
resign the case and return my money. I did not do so earlier because
you were recommended by a mutual friend, and because of the
additional burden of time and expense involved in my finding a
new lawyer.

Thinking that perhaps my expectations from you were not
within the standards of lawyer/client relations in Germany, I called
the Legal Department of the German Embassy for advice. Their
answer was, "You should have fired him sooner."

I will be in Berlin on February 23/24. I would appreciate it if
you could a have check ready for 1000 DM, the sum I paid you
as an advance at the time I retained you. I will call your office on
my arrival to work out the time when I may come by to pick up
the check.

P.S. Your reference on the phone to HJ is taken out of context and
unjustified. Unlike you, HJ does not speak English. However, in
my more then twenty years of association with him he has given
generously of himself and gone out of his way to accommodate me,

in spite of the fact that he and I did not have a common language in which I could articulate my concerns.

The visit to my grandfather's house, the imminent reunification of Germany, and the prospect of contact and possible conflict with my uncle's children over the house raised emotional and practical concerns that brought me to conclude that I may have put HJ in a difficult position vis à vis my uncle's children.

I thought having a lawyer with whom I shared a common language might also relieve some of the emotional strain of these issues. That was the reason, and the sole reason, I came to you.

Sincerely,
Peter Paz

Nice, France, February 1993

Dear Joe:

I just got back from Berlin, this time to fire my Israeli lawyer, DB, and rehire my old German lawyer, HJ, whom I fired the last time I went to Berlin to hire DB, all in my effort to get back my German citizenship. You are right to laugh. I would too if it wasn't so sad. I guess I may have to go back to Israel to eventually get the passport thing straightened out. Beverly really wants to go.

We talked about it before going to sleep last night. Something stirred in me during my sleep, I must have wanted to please her. That night I had a dream. In my dream, I am arriving at Israel's Lod International Airport as a dog.

"He must first go into quarantine," I hear the Immigration Officer say, looking at my papers.

"He's a poodle!" Beverly says, "living on the Cote d'Azur." Panic is working its way up my tail, for the next line I am certain she is going to bring up my nails. "Look at his nails, they look better than yours," or lift me up, stick me in his face and say something like, "What do you think he has? He looks better than you!" But she doesn't.

"This dog," she says instead, "is from Nice, Officer, the capital of the French Riviera! Dog's paradise on earth." If the officer is impressed, he doesn't show it.

"How long has he lived there? Are you his original owner? Where did he live before? And before that? And before that?"

The more questions he asks the more convinced I become that this is all a mistake, that we should turn around, go back, forget all about this vacation.

"We are going to take him in," says the Immigration official.

"But why," she protests, pulling at my leash.

"It's the law!" I hear him say. "You see, Madam Pimsleur, since you are not his original owner, you don't even know whether he is really a poodle," the Officer says, tightening his lips.

"What are you talking about?" she interrupts him, stretching herself another inch or so, raising her voice.

"He can be anything, Madam, another dog, even a *person* for all we know! You have no idea what people won't do to get into the country these days," he says in a somewhat defensive, lecturing tone, betraying his clean-shaven clerical appearance.

Knowing Beverly's temper I am prepared for the worst. I am waiting for her to say "My 84-year-old father, bless his soul, has been raising money all his life to plant trees in your country. Do you have any idea what it takes to make Americans (no longer rich) to part with money, in communities surrounded by TOYS 'R US and video arcades, humming like wounded whales twenty-four hours a day?"

But when her voice comes out she is a pussycat—Southern-sweet and mellow. "Look Officer, what do you need a little poodle for?"

"Well, Madam," the officer says, responding in kind, "if he is really a poodle we may let him go. But I will be frank with you, he may not be a poodle after all."

"I thought we were through with this," she says, her temper rising again.

"I know, but my computer is flashing a message, Madam. Would you like to see it?"

Incredulous, she rolls her eyes.

"File for a Peter Paz," he reads.
Born: Berlin
Date: 8/31/1937
Aliya*: March 27, 1946
Current Address, unknown.

"Do you know what "Aliya*" is, Madam? He asks in a grave muted tone.

"Yes I do," she says through her teeth.

"We are going to hold him, Madam."

"On what charge, if I may ask?"

"You may, but we don't have to tell you."

"I am an American citizen," she says, her voice rising.

---

* Aliya is a term used to mean Jewish immigration to Israel. It is a concept that permits any Jew the legal right to assisted immigration and settlement in Israel, as well as automatic Israeli citizenship.

He cuts her off (before she can do any real damage) saying, "This, Madam, is Israel!" I was sure she is going to say: "Without us you wouldn't be here!" and I begin to pray, please don't let her say that.

"How long?" she asks.

"Until we get the details of his file."

"And how long will that take?" her temper is rising with the sun.

"It can take a day, a week, I can't really say."

"A week!" I hear her blurt out. "But I only have a week," she says in a piercing voice.

"All of Israel in a week," I hear him mumble to himself. "If you will tell us what we need to know we may not need to hold him that long." That was the line the East German Security Police laid on me when they picked me up, on suspicions that I had photographed the Kremlin's entourage arriving to boot Herr Ulbricht out of office.

"Like what?" she asks, as though she has nothing to hide. She has always suspected that I was a spy. Me, with my Swiss cheese memory . . . !

"Did he come by plane or boat?"

"We came on Sabena flight 78," she says.

"I know that Madam. I mean *him*," he says looking her straight in the eyes.

"Him," she says in astonishment. "How on earth am I supposed to know that? I have only had him for 12 years."

"Twelve years is a long time, Madam," he says pausing dramatically. "I thought he may have told you."

"He is a *dog*, officer."

"I know," he says. "We have been through this before."

"I think he came by boat," I hear her say. "What's the difference?" She is beginning to wilt, I can tell.

"It's cheaper by boat," he says.

"Cheaper?" she cries in surprise and exasperation. "He is not cheap! He has never done anything cheap. But I don't think he paid for his ticket, Officer."

"Nobody paid for his ticket then. That's the trouble," he says reflectively. "Even today, no one pays."

"Pays for what, Officer?" She interrupts him again.

"For the costs of being brought here, Madam."

"Please don't call me, Madam," she says tartly, the curl in the middle of her forehead beginning to rise. "You are talking about more than forty years ago, forty-seven to be exact, he was eight years old."

"Where did he go when he came?"

"A kibbutz."

"What kibbutz?"

"I don't know, what difference does it make?"

"All the difference in the world. Madam. We will be able to trace him."

"I will tell you one thing officer, he didn't really like it there."

"How do you know?"

"He told me."

"Told you?"

"Yes."

"What else did he tell you?"

"He said he had never heard of Palestine. Didn't know you existed, didn't ask to be brought here. He asked for America."

"Everyone does, Madam. When my father brought us here from Casablanca, we lived in a one-room tin shack on a bare mountain in Kiryat Shemona. All eight of us, for 11 years, Madam! In one room! Those Ashkenazim gave us hell. Do you think we liked it? Now it's our turn."

"But I thought every Jew was welcome."

"Some more than others," he says with a thin smile. "And provided they can prove they are Jewish."

"And what if they didn't ask to be bought here, like my dog?"

"All the same, Madam, they must pay. It's the law. Can you imagine how many hard luck stories there are in this country? Can you imagine the scene of listening to everyone's story?"

The way things are going, I lower my head as low as I can, kind of folding into myself, and try not to get morbid when I hear the Officer's voice asking, "Do you think he (referring to me) is okay?"

I freeze in my tracks, trying not to breathe and keeping my ears from dragging on the ground. "He is just sulking," she says with affection, concern and a dash of guilt. "He does that sometimes."

"I don't know," the Officer says, clearly skeptical.

"I really feel awful," I hear her say in her best reflective tone. I could tell, without lifting my head to look at her, that she is shaking her head as she says it, repeating it over and over, "He really did not want to come."

"I know," says the Officer without sympathy.

"No you don't," she says. I am not talking about then, she says nearly in tears. "I am talking about now, officer. I tricked him! Took him against his will. I feel just awful."

"Do you know Madam, whether he served in the Army?" I hold my breath. But she just stares at him, saying nothing.

"He may owe us a lot of "milueem" service," he says as he reflects.

"What's milueem?" she demands to know.

"Service in the military reserves."

"But he is a poodle," she reminds him, half pleading, exasperated, "fifty-five years old!"

"That, Madam, remains to be seen," says he. "Besides, put in the right environment even a poodle can become a fighter, and, as I am sure you know, we need every . . . Just then, I woke up.

My love to Mildred and the group.

Love, Peter

Editor's Note: Peter made a first trip alone to Israel in the spring of 1994 in order to begin the process of reactivating his Israeli passport. He stayed with his cousin, Miriam's younger brother David, his wife and children on their kibbutz.

CHAPTER 8

THE PASSPORT STORY

Nice, 1994

On hearing that I would be going to Israel Luba was surprised. As far as she knew it was not in the cards, at least for now. When I told her that I was going to renew my Israeli passport so that I could renew my German citizenship, she paused, long enough to take a breath then said, "The clock of your life is running backward."

Just before boarding my flight, I discovered that I was holding a ticket for Nice—Rome—Tel Aviv, Tel Aviv—Rome—Nice written for "Mr. Pimsleur," Beverly's late husband. I boarded the plane anyway thinking that no one would notice it in Nice, which they didn't. But in Rome there had been a highjacking attempt just before lunchtime. There was nothing I could do but hope for the best.

The final boarding call for Alitalia's flight to Tel Aviv came after four hours of waiting, announcements, retractions, and much to-dos. At the gate, there were five security guards. The first, second, and third let me though, but the fourth asked for my passport. After close to an hour of retelling my story—in French—that Beverly's travel agent, who should have known better, had accidentally put her last name on my ticket instead of mine, they let me board the flight.

It took less than five minutes after landing at Lod Airport to realize that, except for the posters promoting travel in Israel, it hadn't changed since I left in 1963. With all the talk of how much Israel had changed, I was surprised.

After speaking with Israelis in Israel during my visit, I had the distinct impression most of them hold two separate realities in their minds, two different sets of pictures of the country. In the first set, the country is depicted by official-speak. In the second set are the pictures in which their real life is staring back at them. In reading the Israeli press, current literature, and in conversations with Israelis, one gets the impression that after so many years of government by nationalist hype, Israelis are no longer able to tell the difference between the fake reality of self-congratulation and the nightmare they keep denying with righteous indignation.

By demonizing any opposition to their policies, the fathers of Zionism, who were no democrats, have successfully eliminated all that was essential for their movement of national renewal from becoming a religion. Orthodox Zionism has been so successful in demonizing non-Zionist opposition, that today anti-Zionism means not merely being opposed to a Zionist state, but being opposed to the very idea of Jews having a right to a homeland—and worse, being an anti-Semite. But as Yosele points out, individual Israelis are as insecure in their streets, in their homes, as their great-grandfathers were in the shtetles of Russia or Poland.

At the heart of Israel's predicament lies an Orwellian democracy, built upon fear of "the other," fear of coexistence with the Palestinians, which the founding fathers viewed as the beginning of the end of the Jewish state.

In Israel's early years, it was hoped that the resolution of the conflict with the Palestinians would bring peace to Israeli society. Instead, racial, religious, and economic conflicts have been winning for most of the last forty-seven years. Even if the Palestinian threat recedes, old unresolved conflicts will keep any peace dividends from most Israelis.

For most of this century, conflict has been woven into the fabric that today makes up Israeli society. It is a society in which one of the most serious conflicts has yet to be resolved: the redistribution of internal resources and political power between the majority of Jews from Spain, North Africa and the Middle East and the minority of Ashkenazy Jews, who for the last forty-odd years have systematically kept the Jews of Edot HaMizrah economically down and out of power.

Most Israelis I spoke to said, "We are sleeping with one eye open, we would be crazy not to," which is the kindest thing I heard said about the government. The mood here is cool detachment, observers unfamiliar may take it for indifference. But it is anything but. It is, of course, the good old-fashioned mode of denial, necessary to keep oneself going, in spite of everything.

Incidents in which the Israeli Defense Forces kill Palestinians now occur daily. Today's case is the headline of every newspaper because those killed were key members of the PLO security force, essential for putting in place the first stage of the peace process. Is the government losing control of the army? Given the "incident" that occured during Passover week, it is not unreasonable to think so. A massive manhunt, mounted by the army three days ago in Hebron, netted four suspected members of Hamas. That six key members of the PLO security apparatus were killed on the eve of the renewal of the peace process is puzzling, given that the press, from the Right to the Left, suggests that it may further complicate the resumption of the peace process.

FLIGHT BACK: From Tel Aviv to Rome

"What did you expect?" asked the woman sitting next to me when I said that I was disappointed at what I found.

"I expected to see what I have been told by Israelis for years, that the country has changed so much, you will not recognize it."

"I don't know what you are talking about," she said, withdrawing into herself, pursing her lips.

"I was going to hit you for the thing you said before," she said later, in an accented English, after downing half a bottle of Chianti with lunch.

The traces of a flaming beauty were all about her. She was born in one of the oldest kibbutzim of Emek Israel, married an Englishman, and in 1952 moved to England, where she had five children. She was a grandmother now, "a flying Granny," she said, living in orderly Monte Carlo, surrounded by peace and money. And was dressed for the part.

"But I don't hit passengers who tell me disagreeable things, even lies," she continued.

"Then why did you want to hit me?" I replied.

"Because you are not a friend of Israel."

"If by a friend of Israel, you mean one of those silent Americans who keep footing the bill for every kind of Israeli folly, then I am certainly no friend of Israel."

"What kind of folly do you mean?"

"Since you and I behold a very different country, it would be pointless to speak to you of this or that folly. But I would like to leave you with something to think about. Before Ariel Sharon launched the invasion of Lebanon, he requested permission to launch a nuclear attack on Syria. Begin turned him down. Given Begin's state of mind at the time, he could just as well have given Sharon the green light. If you are the friend of Israel you say you are, I would like you to imagine the fallout of launching such an attack. And while you are at it, you might reflect on the nature of a government that would saddle a population of 1.5 million with the costs of developing a nuclear arsenal—not to mention the risk of it being used. I doubt that you would ever do so, because the implication of such an act would inevitably lead most women of reason to cast doubt on the government, its reliability, the judgment, and accountability of its officials to the voters. In a democratic society, government can no longer govern when it loses the respect of the electorate."

"Passing judgment on what Israelis do is easy when one lives in New York," she retorted, angrily.

"I am not passing judgment on Israelis, I am passing it on the policy and record of the Israeli government. That you should confuse the two is not surprising, most Israelis do. They do because the founding fathers spoke of democracy, but their instinct about government was rooted in the traditions of Russia and Poland. Ben-Gurion did not trust the public's judgment. The Israeli government has always cloaked its doings with the national flag, and denied the publics' right to know. Of all western-style democracies, the Israelis are the only ones to have no free access to information that affects their security and daily lives because it is restricted by their government, and information has become the creation of the state."

"And are Israelis today more secure then they were?" I asked her. "Are Israelis—white, black, Arabs—better educated? And what does the future hold for young Israelis?"

"Do you really think that living in New York or Nice as you have, gives you the right to pass judgment?" she retorted, angrily.

I have heard the same question, phrased the same way so often, by so many Israelis that it no longer seemed practical to ignore it. "The problem with your question is that you ask it as if it was a legitimate question, which, of course, it is not. It is part of the Zionist dogma. It may well have been legitimate response to those who criticized Israel when the war against the Palestinians was a local war, a war between the Israelis and their neighbors. Today that war is no longer an internal affair of Israel. Leon Klinghoffer was not thrown overboard from the *Achilli Lauro* because he was sitting in a wheelchair. He became a target because he was considered to be a part of a community of Americans whose unquestioned economic, military, and political support of Israel's war against the Palestinians had become a factor in that war, a crucial factor. So when Israel lobbies for support, as it does on Capitol Hill, de facto, it is asking every American taxpayer to become a potential target. As an American I, too, have become a potential target, because of the military and economic aid that Israel receives from America. You may hit me if you wish, but I am not going to take that spiel."

"What spiel?" she asked.

"That I have no right to say what's on my mind. It may shock you, but not only do I have a right, I have an *obligation*. My "right" resides in the heart of the American idea that taxation without representation is unjust and unacceptable. As a Jew, I have an obligation to tell you the truth, what is on my mind, because your government is either unwilling, or unable to tell you. And as a survivor of the Holocaust, I am heartsick to see what Jewish nationalism has done to what the National Tourist Office still refers to as "The Dream." In the last forty-seven years, Israelis have been preoccupied with issues of survival and legitimacy. Israeli writers like Amos Oz, David Grossman, and A. B. Yehoshua have been addressing the question of internal conflict. Why have most Jews, given the chance, chosen to go anywhere but to Israel? Would you like to know what I think?"

"Not really, but there are no free seats on the plane."

Once we landed, she got up and left without speaking. She seemed uneasy about missing her Monte Carlo connection. As they say in Monte Carlo, "Money comes and money goes, but guilt is forever."

Attention: Mr. Jurgens
Consulate Generale de la Republic Federal d'Allemagne
Marseille, France
AZ: RK 515 Goldman
4/5/1995

Dear Mr. Jurgens:

When you first offered to help me locate a copy of my birth certificate, I was unaware of the regulation you cite in your letter of 3/10/1995. The implication of the cited regulation is that I am not entitled to a passport because I do not possess a birth certificate. I am, therefore, unable to accept your offer, for acceptance would imply acceptance of the said regulation.

I was arrested by the Gestapo when I was 4 or 5 years old, along with my mother. By the time the Russians liberated my camp, every member of my immediate family, except for my maternal grandmother, was dead.

Though I do not for a moment doubt the sincerity of your offer, I doubt that the regulation you cite is intended to deny me a passport. Such an interpretation would raise doubts about Germany's avowed aim of atoning for the Nazi regime's crimes against humanity.

I will be leaving in a few weeks for an assignment in the Middle East. If you are unable to issue me a passport, would you please be so kind as to have my application forwarded to Tel Aviv, so I will be able to take this matter up with the German consul when I am there.

I thank you again.

Sincerely, Peter Paz

CC: Mr. Dirk Ludigkeit, attaché, Embassy of the Federal Republic of Germany, Tel Aviv

Attention: Mr. Jurgens
Consulate Generale de la Republic Federal d'Allemagne

Dear Mr. Jurgens:

I was upset to learn that you understood my critical reference to your government's policy to reflect on you personally. I want to reassure you, in no uncertain terms, that no such inference was intended.

I was and remain very grateful for your concern and good will in this matter.

Sincerely yours,
Yigal Paz
Peter Paz/Peter S. Goldman

Editor's Note: Peter made a second trip to Israel with Beverly in the summer of 1995 when he was issued an Israeli passport, giving him the right to request a German one. He finally received the much-awaited German passport in 1995, after more than five years of frustrating dealings with different lawyers and consulates.

7/11/1995
Attention: Mrs. Prevost
Consulate Generale de la Republic Federal d'Allemagne
338 Ave. du Prado 13008
Marseille, France

Dear Mrs. Prevost:

I was away when my passport arrived in the mail. I want you to know that your understanding and goodwill has made a more meaningful contribution in my effort to reconstruct my life than I could possibly express in words. I am profoundly grateful.

Sincerely, Peter Paz/Peter S. Goldman

The same letter was sent to Mr. Jurgens.

December 1997

Dear Joe:

Hello there,

Tried to get connected by email in France with three different discs from London, but none worked. It's been a mess. Probably has to do with the English insistence on being English, like driving on the wrong side of the road.

I finally gave up on Compuserve, Beverly's server, as well. So I'm back to letters.

People get silly around the end of the year. Which is the only way I can explain why I accepted a registered letter from the German Consulate, a week before Christmas. Written in official German from the German Senate in Berlin was a letter, informing me that I have been stripped by the Senate of my nationality. An attached note from the Marseille Consulate demanded that I return my nationality papers and passport to them immediately, signed "Mit Freundlichen Grusen" (friendly greetings), Iris Schirra.

I took a very deep breath. Then took a long walk up to the Chateau, kicking myself every step on the way for breaking a rule never to accept a registered letter from Germany. When I came down, I called the Consulate and asked to speak with Madame Prevost, who has been an island of humanity in a world of clerks, a source of support and help in my six-year effort to regain my German nationality.

"Madame Prevost is dead," said a woman on the line.

I identified myself and asked to speak to Ms. Schirra.

"I am Ms. Schirra," said the woman.

"I am calling in response to your recent correspondence," I told Ms. Schirra. "I am unable to respond to your correspondence since I do not speak or read German."

"There is nothing to understand," said Ms. Schirra, "we simply want you to return your passport and nationality papers immediately. Of course, I will not.

Received a form from my lawyer advising me to keep watching for the latest news of the Swiss and their Nazi gold. Beverly and I spent the evening looking through the family pictures for gold, silver, jewelry, and art. Found a picture of my mother wearing a necklace of pearls. The picture of her at the piano disappeared from my Hell's Kitchen apartment along with my collection of Billie Holiday records after a break-in years ago. Again Happy New Year and much love to you both,

Yigal and Beverly

Attention: Mr. Densch V. Consul
Consulate Generale de la Republic Federal d'Allemagne
338 Ave. du Prado
13008 Marseille, France

Regarding:
My request for a translation of the mail received from your office: Dec.
1/ Dec. 3/ and December 11, 1997 concerning my nationality and
Passport.

Dear Mr. Densch:

I am profoundly troubled by the casual, off-hand tone of the above correspondence, as if the matter at hand was an every-day routine affair, rather than the stripping of one's nationality, and the right thereunder, by the "Senatsverwaltung."*

That off-hand, clipped, dry tone reminded me of the letter the Gestapo sent to Magdalena Goldmann, my grandmother, just months before the end of the war. It was a note, informing her that her daughter, Dorothea Goldmann, my mother, held by the Gestapo for 18 months, had died in Ravensbruk. That letter, too, was signed, "Mit freundlichen Grusen."

I called Ms. Schirra to explain that since I do not speak or read German, I could not possibly respond to her correspondence. I asked that she send me an English translation, at her convenience. She replied, "There is nothing to understand. We simply want you to send us your German passport."

Given that the right to a nationality and the rights there under are accepted as a basic human right, *inalienable rights* in most enlightened liberal democracies these days, I take the view that the Senatsverwaltung's decision to strip me of my German nationality was a political act that, in fact, exceded its authority under the German constitution. And, therefore, the issue at hand is an issue of a basic human right, to be decided not by the Senatsverwaltung but by the Constitutional Court.

---

*   German senate administration

It is, therefore, essential that I be provided with a full translation of all correspondence, documents, and minutes relating to the said process and the final decision by the Senatsverwaltung as soon as possible.

As I do not have the means to pursue this matter, I ask that I be provided with an English-speaking lawyer, competent in constitutional law, to represent my case.

Respectfully,
Peter S. Goldman

Reference: RK 512.21 Goldman
Attention: Ms. Brigit Densch, Vice Consul
Consulate Generale de la Republic Federale d'Allemagne
Re: The Senatsverwaltung action to strip me of my German
nationality and passport.

Dear Ms. Densch:

It is over six weeks since I have requested and that you have
assured me that I would receive a complete and detailed English
translation of the Senatsverwaltung decision to cancel, lift or strip
me, if you will, of my nationality and German passport granted
me in November of 1994.

I believe that the Senatsverwaltung action contradicts the
Federal Administrative Court's ruling of January 11/1994 that
all the descendants of tens of thousands of Germans—mainly
Jews—who were driven into exile by the Nazis and stripped of their
citizenship had the right to take up German nationality again. In
its decision The Federal Administrative Court said: "The decision
was in keeping with Germany's avowed aim of atoning for the Nazi
regime's crimes against humanity."

Since I have been kept completely and deliberately in the dark
about the Senate's decision and what brought it about, I am obliged
to reserve any response to your requests, beyond stating the obvious:
The Senatsverwaltung action has effectively rendered me subject to
deportation from France. Surely the German government does not
expect me to become an accomplice to my own deportation.

Sincerely,
Peter S. Goldmann

CC. The World Jewish Congress
Joseph Katz Phd.
Alfonse M. D' Amato Senate New York
THE WILLIAM MARKS LAW FIRM, Washington D.C

Attention: Mr. Hansen, Consul
Consulate Generale de la Republic Federal d'Allemagne
Feb. 2, 1998

Re: RK 512.21 Goldmann

Dear Mr. Hansen:

I fully comprehend the fact that the consulate in Marseille is not competent to translate the Berlin Senate's decision, mentioned in your letter of Jan 23. 1998. What I do not comprehend is why, in its rush to strip me of my citizenship, nationality and passport, the German Senate did not see fit to respect my constitutional, political and civil rights. "In a society that respects human rights under the rule of law, the individual is entitled that the law will recognize him as having rights and obligations, and will treat him equally with all others, whoever he is and however powerful those others may be.

He will likewise expect that any legal dispute in which he becomes involved, whether as a claimant or as a respondent to someone else's claim, and whether against another individual, or a corporation, or a trade union, or the state itself—will be adjudicated by fair procedures, in courts and by judges that are impartial and independent, and that he will there have equality of arms with his opponent, and such legal assistance and representation as he may need . . ." Paul Sieghart, *The Lawful Right of Mankind": An introduction to the International Legal Code of Human Rights*, Oxford University Press New York, 1985.

The last seven years of my dealings with the Consulate, I believe, have been based on mutual respect, professionalism and good will. We have had our differences, but at no time did I have cause to doubt Germany's commitment to the rule of law and to the survivors of the Holocaust.

The Consulate's handling of this affair, however, from Ms. Schirra's rude response to my original telephone inquiry regarding the above, to Ms. Densch's deliberate misstatement that I refused to correspond in German or in French, to the Berlin Senate's continued stonewalling of my requests for a translation of its decision, I am sorry to say, shatters that belief.

QUESTIONS

1) Who initiated the process that led the Berlin Senate to vote, and why?

2) Why, nearly two months after your Vice Consul Ms. Densch's reassurance that I would be receiving a full and detailed English translation of the Senate's vote, have I not received it.

3) How did the Berlin Senate come to vote on my nationality without my being informed about it?

4) Who initiated the process that led the Berlin senate to vote on my nationality and why was I not informed of the fact?

5) Given that at stake in the Berlin senate's decision was my birthright to German nationality, why was I not informed until 8 weeks after the vote was taken?

6) Regarding the vote about destitution, the subject at hand, why was I not provided with a document I could comprehend in the first place?

The most troubling of all has been the inelegant communications and deliberate inaction marked by gratuitous ill will. I would very much like to attribute this to inexperience and poor training, rather then to an expression of a new German policy with respect to elementary human rights, including the rights of German Jews and survivors of the Holocaust regarding their rights to nationality, habeas corpus, citizen's right to know, and to the principle that government is accountable to its citizens for its actions.

I thank you.

Sincerely, Peter Paz

October 13, 1998

Dear Howard:*

To begin with, I want you to know how profoundly touched and deeply grateful I am at your interest in this issue and willingness to pursue it. Here is the shortened version of my attempt to obtain a German passport.

In 1990, we decided to move to Europe and spend part of every year living and working there. This necessitated European citizenship papers for me in order to work legally in the EEC countries. I assumed that Germany could hardly refuse me a passport, since I spent the war years in a concentration camp where I lost my immediate family. So I approached the German consulate in NY in the spring of '90 about reinstating my German citizenship.

The 20-year-old clerk, after making sure that my American passport was in order, started leafing through the Book of Laws. He seemed to know what he was looking for. He said, "Well, you lost your German nationality and citizenship when you left Germany." "You mean in 1945?" I asked. "Yes," he replied. "But I was eight, living on the street and my immediate family was dead." "I am very sorry," he said, "but that is all I can tell you."

We left a few months later for Berlin, where I decided to try and hire a lawyer to deal with the problem from there. A decision had been announced in 1994 by the Federal Administration Court to grant citizenship to the grandchildren of a family who fled Germany in 1932. "The decision," the court said "was in keeping with Germany's avowed aim of atoning for the Nazi regime's crimes against humanity." So I thought it would not be difficult to work through Germany.

After five years, four lawyers, four trips to Berlin and considerable expense, I received a call from my then current lawyer, who said: "I can give you good news. Your German nationality was never cancelled. I can get your German passport and nationality re-instated. But there is one problem. I would have to state to the Minister of the Interior that you are not an American citizen, which

---

*   Dr. Howard Sloan, husband of Beverly's friend Elaine Sloan

as a lawyer, I cannot do. But *you* can go to Tel Aviv with your Israeli passport and apply at the German Consulate for the reinstatement of your German nationality."

In 1994-95 I made two trips to Tel Aviv to try and accomplish this. Three months after my last trip, I received a note from the German Consulate to say: "Your German passport and nationality certificate are ready for you in Marseille."

I called Madame Prevost, the German Vice-Consul who had supported my effort from the very beginning. "How does it feel to have three passports, under three different names,'" she asked. I heard myself say, "A Jew cannot have too many passports."

A few days before Christmas in 1997, I received a registered letter in German from the Consul in Marseille. Since I did not fully understand the contents, I called and asked to speak with Madame Prevost. "She's dead," said the woman on the other end of the line. I then asked to speak to Madame Schirra, the one who signed the document. "I am Madame Schirra," said the woman on the line. I identified myself and said I was calling about the recent correspondence that I did not fully understand since I did not speak or read German. "There is nothing to understand, Mr. Paz," said Madame Schirra. "We simply want you to return your German passport and nationality papers, immediately."

The registered letter from the Senatsverwaltung Berlin—a parliamentary committee as far as I could figure out—said that I had been stripped of my nationality. The accompanying note from the Consulate demanded that I return the passport and nationality certificate to this office. It was signed by Mrs. Schirra "Mit freundlichen Grussen."

I subsequently requested a full English translation of the document so that I could respond to it. It was promised to be sent, but has never arrived. I called the Consul and told him that without a complete translation of the letter sent by the Senatsverwaltung, I was completely in the dark about their decision and what brought it about. You will see by the correspondence enclosed that the Consul informed me, after my request for legal representation, that I could

<hr />

*   Yigal Paz, Peter Paz, Peter Sigmund Goldmann

apply for a court-appointed lawyer to challenge the decision IF I could prove financial need. I am in the process of doing this.

The decision to strip me of my German nationality and passport two years after issuing it is a clear contradiction of the Federal Administrative Court's ruling that the descendants of tens of thousands of Germans—mainly Jews who were driven into exile by the Nazis and stripped of their citizenship—had the right to take up German nationality again.

In its decision the Federal Administrative Court said: "The decision was in keeping with Germany's avowed aim of atoning for the Nazi regime's crimes against humanity."

During the experience of having my passport and citizenship given back to me, I have hardly noticed that the way I've been dealt has been an attempt to "atone" for anything. On the contrary, (and this is also true of my eight-year unsuccessful attempt to re-possess my grandfather's house, business and property in East Berlin), I have often been made to feel like a criminal, undeserving and forced to defend myself against the authorities. I have also been asked to furnish information that could not possibly be in my possession, in a language which is not my own, since schooling was denied me by the Germans, who are now shocked that I can't communicate in their language.

I hope this is not too incoherent. I also have copies of my correspondence with the German consulate, copies of my various passports, etc. If you need them, I'll overnight them to you.

Obviously, if you need anything else in any other form, please email Beverly.

Warmest regards,
Peter

Editor's note: Howard, though he tried, was not able to help Peter either. Peter, after many inquiries, finally received a response from the German consulate in Marseille in 1999, saying that because he was also an American citizen, he did not have the right to be a German citizen. He was unsuccessful in his attempt to convince the German consul in France to provide him with a court lawyer to represent him to appeal the decision. His German passport and citizenship were never re-instated.

CHAPTER 9

GRANDFATHER'S HOUSE

Editor's Note: Cousin Miriam

From the time Miriam London first wrote to Peter in 1993, they corresponded regularly, catching up with each other's lives. They exchanged news of their families; Miriam and her husband Joe had two children, a daughter, Zoey and a son, David, who came for a visit to Nice with his new wife in the winter of 1995. But the main topic of the letters and faxes between Miriam and Peter was the subject of their grandfather's house, and how to go about reclaiming it. In this they had different, and eventually, conflicting opinions.

In the summer of 1995, Miriam came to visit Peter and Beverly in Nice. Although the visit was anticipated with enthusiasm by all, the several issues between them put a strain on their relationship. The main source of contention was who should represent them legally in their attempt to reclaim the Rosswein property. Before her visit, Miriam had sent Peter information from Australia about an Australian lawyer, Kelleher, who had successfully represented claims for other Jewish families. Since neither Peter nor Miriam were confident that WM would pursue their case aggressively, Peter, with Miriam's consent, had contacted Kelleher. Miriam did not want to participate in the lawyer's fees and Peter agreed to pay them, with the understanding that if the claim was resolved, he would be reimbursed. Peter then engaged Kelleher, who proceeded to investigate the case.

However, when Miriam arrived in Nice, she told Peter that her uncle on her mother's side had dissuaded her from joining the Kelleher claim with Peter because she, Miriam, had another separate claim for her mother's house. Her uncle thought she should let the two be handled by the same person, in this case, Herrn Theuerkauf, who represented the German organization, URO (United Restitution Organization); Peter was upset by this change of plans and tried unsuccessfully to change Miriam's mind.

Another subject of Peter's concern was why Miriam's father hadn't requested the kibbutz to send Peter to Australia, once it was discovered that Peter was alive. Miriam insisted that her father had tried to do just that, but the kibbutz had replied that they were better equipped to deal with traumatized war orphans. Peter was not entirely convinced by this explanation, since he had heard nothing from his Uncle Rudolf from the time his grandmother first wrote to him when he was thirteen, until his uncle, aunt and their younger son, David, appeared at the kibbutz when Peter was twenty-one. During Miriam's visit, she revealed that her mother never did adjust to the harsh circumstances of life as an immigrant in Australia and suffered severe bouts of depression which necessitated her hospitalization. When Peter considered that he might have spent his teen years in the family of his uncle, he confided to Beverly that perhaps he had been fortunate, after all, to have remained on the kibbutz. For that is where he was encouraged to dance, leading to a career, which he said, was one of the most satisfying and joyful parts of his life.

THE CORRESPONDENCE

Nice, France, 1994

Dear Miriam:

I have not been to Israel since I left in 1962. I plan to go back to Israel this spring to get the passport situation figured out.

I finally got through to WM's office (after firing DB and re-hiring WM) about the status of my German citizenship. WM has had my citizenship case on his desk for over four years, and it would have been there for another forty years if I had not called him every few months to ask, "How is it going?" This time I called out of politeness, before, as you say, "sacking" him. I had his assistant, WM, on the phone, telling me: "We have a problem. Thank God," I thought to myself, "we are making progress!"

"What is the problem?" I asked.

"Well," said WM. "We know you are an American citizen. In order to get your citizenship we will have to lie. Do you understand?" I stopped for a moment thinking: "Why did it take four years to tell me that?!" For a moment I was tempted to say "Your people did far worse than lie taking my citizenship." But there was no point, it was irrelevant. WM wasn't even born when that bloody business was going on.

"Of course I understand," I said, thanking him for being candid. So I'll be going to Israel.

Writing this letter has been on my mind since August. Every time I sit down to write, determined to make sense out of our predicament regarding Grandfather's house, WM, and what Germany is or is not going to do about Jewish properties in the East, my mind begins to drift. I feel confounded by the realization that it is a loaded issue for all and that few are prepared to deal with, unless the property is large enough for a lawyer to sink his teeth in.

At the recommendation of Stan Goldberg, a multimedia specialist and friend from New York who was staying with us in September, I have made contact with a lawyer in Hamburg.* This lawyer negotiated Stan's contract with a German company engaged to develop a multimedia center for the city of Cologne. I had two long telephone conversations with the lawyer about my claim for reinstating my German citizenship. He sounds like the right lawyer—all business, tough, listens, responds, and follows up on questions put to him.

Beverly's father has cancer of the lymph-nodes, so she went to Columbus for a month to be with him. Between making pots of chicken soup she contacted a lawyer** who was hired by her cousin's family to go after an old factory in East Germany (lots of money). He could not take our case but said there was an American legal organization that was paid a lump sum to compensate German Jews for lost property.

I have not contacted them for information; first, because we didn't discuss it; second, because I suspect it is for American citizens; and third, because I suspect it will be the same take it or leave it deal all institutions (German, British, Australian or Israeli) will offer.

In my conversation with the Hamburg lawyer I did ask if his firm has the expertise to handle our claim should we ask him to. He assured me that they do.

Given the rate at which the value of property in and around Berlin is going, it would be foolhardy to accept a symbolic token (nowhere near its market value) for the property at this time. All things being equal, my opinion is that we will do best to claim the property and then consider our options. Take your time and let me know what you think.

Love and all the best,

Your cousin,
Peter

---

* The Hamburg lawyer was hired by Peter, but like DB, he did not actively pursue the claim. Peter replaced him with an American lawyer, William Marks, who did not make much progress with the case either.

** Beverly's conversation with Max Osen: He said he did not think there would be a rapid resolution of the claim. He asked if Peter had children, as he thought Peter's daughter, in her lifetime, might receive something.

FAX TO: WM and/or HJ

Dear HJ:

I am profoundly troubled to learn that my claim to Alfons Goldmann's house has been submitted to the Landratsamt* Dobeln, (L.D.). I do not recall being consulted or informed of your intention to submit this matter to an administrative resolution in what was once East Germany. Whatever the origins of the Dobeln institution, the tone and style of the L.D. decision betray the hallmarks of a government consistent with the concept of modern democracy. The fact that the jurisdiction in question is part of the former DDR, a region rife with extreme right-wing violence, can hardly inspire confidence in the L.D.

I, therefore, ask that you undertake to inform the L.D. as well as Mr. Peter Ginter, that this mater has been submitted to the L.D. without my knowledge or consent, and of my intention to take legal actions aimed at overturning the ruling.

To facilitate this undertaking, I ask that the L.D. provide me with all transcripts of their deliberations, all reference documents relevant to their decision, including a full text and origin, of the laws they cited as the foundation for their decision, in either Hebrew or English.

I also ask that the L.D. provide all documents, and records of the transactions between Alfons Goldman and Bruno Max Taubert, as well as all records of the transaction between Bruno Max Taubert, his wife, and or children, and Peter Ginter, the present owner, in either Hebrew or English.

My position in this matter is that, Bruno Max Taubert, a Nazi party member, was a direct beneficiary of the Nazi regime's campaign designed to bring about a Germany without Jews. In other words, the manner by which Bruno Max Taubert gained possession of Alfons Goldman's property is, to say the least, legally questionable.

In my view, Peter Ginter's legal standing is similar to that of a person who buys a painting from a person who obtained the

---

*   district council of town of Dobeln

painting by questionable means. Surely no German court would recognize Peter Ginter as the legal owner of the painting merely because he paid for it.

What distinguished DDR from the Federal Republic of Germany was that it was a model of government by law. On the other side of the Berlin Wall the Federal Government became an example of government of law. The difference between the two forms of government is as profound as can be.

Until shortly before the collapse of the wall, DDR consistently rejected any responsibility for the deeds of the Nazi regime. It is quite possible that the DDR actually passed laws that gave legal sanction to the transaction between Alfons Goldmann and Bruno Max Taubert. After all the very same regime also sanctioned the shooting of citizens for attempting to leave the DDR.

I am well aware of the fact that the tradition of legal services in Germany are different from legal services practiced elsewhere. However, legal representation without communication is impossible, it is a contradiction in terms. As my lawyer, you may not undertake further action without first communicating with me.

Sincerely,

Peter

Fax to Miriam, June 2, 1995

Dear Miriam:

Itineraries are never easy. I am glad you worked yours out, though. The flight time from London to Nice should be around one hour, according to your itinerary it is two hours. Could you double check on the arrival time?

I am looking forward to your coming.

Much love,

Peter

P.S. I faxed Leonie Kelleher a copy of the L.D. decision and the letter from WM. It appears that the L.D. ruling against my request to get possession of grandfather's house contained a request asking me to respond to their decision within 10 days or two weeks. WM, however, did not mail the document until two or three days before the response was due.

Kelleher's observations were as follows:

1. She thought WM was unbelievably negligent.
2. She thought that LD'S request for my input was unusual and significant, indicating that there must be legal wrinkles that might mitigate against their decision to reject my petition.

She recommended the following:

1. That her legal colleagues from Berlin go to Dobeln, look into the file, examine the particular reasons they gave for rejecting my request and ask to reopen the case. She sounded optimistic about the chances of the case being reopened.
2. That on his way back to Berlin, the lawyer will go to Rosswein and get an estimate of the market value of the house.

After receiving the report from her colleague, she will give me an assessment of our chances of getting title to the house, how long it may take and how much the process may cost. I have also asked her for an estimate of what the Dobeln Landschaft is ready to offer us in compensation in lieu of the house. I expect to have her report sometime after our return from Italy next week.

A P. S. from Beverly

Dear Miriam:

Thank you for your kind and comforting words of sympathy. I appreciate your thinking of me at this difficult time. We're so looking forward to your visit. I know it will be a wonderful opportunity for all of us to get to know each other.

> Love,
> Your new cousin,
> Beverly

September 1995

Dear Joe:

Cousin Miriam's card arrived two years ago saying: "I am your cousin. I have been looking for you for the last twenty-five years." My first impulse was to forget all about it. I have gotten used to doing without family. Seeing what families can do to each other, my inner voice said: you can do without it.

It was two or three years ago that I wrote WM, my lawyer in Berlin saying that I wanted to take possession of my grandfather's house outside Berlin. When I said I I intended to file a request, he first mentioned that I had a Cousin Miriam. I promptly forgot all about it.

After a while, the idea of a real cousin made me think of a kindred spirit to share things one only shares with a therapy group or a family. Who knows, it might work. The more I thought about it the more I came to believe that it would.

Cousin Miriam was due at 10 p.m. Beverly, being a good soul, said, "I am coming with you." It was close to midnight when Cousin Miriam's plane finally landed in Nice. We were both falling off our feet, Cousin Miriam, looking like a Jewish nun, walked through the gate with uneven steps. She had been flying from Menorah, West Australia, to Singapore, to Bangkok, to Bahrain, and onto London, where she stopped for a day to see her 91-year-old aunt. She returned to the airport the following morning, hoping to meet up with her brother, John, and his son Itai, who were to change planes in London on their way from Kibbutz Revivim to Virginia, USA.

On our way home from the airport, I tried to figure out how many hours Cousin Miriam had been in the air. Just thinking about it made me feel dizzy, as if I were the one who had been through this trip. The best I could calculate, Cousin Miriam flew ten hours from Menorah, West Australia, to Singapore, where she had breakfast and bought me a pair of kangaroo socks. "We just can't get them in Menorah," she said. From Singapore Cousin Miriam flew seven hours on to Bahrain, in the Persian Gulf.

"The flight to London was the worst," she said. "I thought it would never end." As best I could figure it, Cousin Miriam was in the air about thirty hours and spent at least six hours on the ground.

At home in the Nice apartment, Cousin Miriam was exhausted. I quietly thanked the Creator and suggested we all go to bed.

While Cousin Miriam slept the next morning, I went to the market determined to make her first dinner in France unforgettable. After leafing through my files of recipes and pictures that would raise a kangaroo up from the dead, I decided to make my old reliable roast chicken, the one with lots of garlic and "herbes de Provence," served with a mush of Provençal summer vegetables, the French call 'ratatouille' and a well-chilled Rosé de Provence.

I was practically out the door when Beverly called out, "I think Cousin Miriam wrote something about being a vegetarian." My roast chicken had by now settled itself in my head, all dressed up in garlic, flapping its wings, anticipating its landing on a plate in a splash of glory. It was so real I could practically smell it. But now there was nothing to do but go on through every one of Cousin Miriam's faxes to discover that Beverly was right, Cousin Miriam was indeed a vegetarian.

Walking past the fruit, vegetables, hanging lambs, goats and wild geese in the market, I tried to talk the roast chicken out of my head in favor of a poached salmon with a light saffron cream sauce. My roast chicken, it seemed, was in no mood to go anywhere. But I couldn't just give in to a roast chicken, it had to go, and that's all there was to it.

I made the poached salmon, with a light saffron cream sauce, with steamed vegetables, boiled potatoes, and a perfectly chilled rosé. Cousin Miriam smiling broadly said, "It's superb."

Cousin Miriam brought with her an old illustrated children's book of German stories and poems, a silver teaspoon and a stack of letters, which she brought out after dessert. When I opened the book I realized it was full of notes, hand-written in pencil. "They were probably made by your mother," I heard Cousin Miriam say." I kept turning the pages mechanically, as if nothing had happened. But the sudden encounter with myself as a child was dizzying.

Some months earlier on the phone, Cousin Miriam had actually told me: "When I was cleaning the attic I found these letters* your mother wrote. I would like to mail them to you but I think they are too fragile." So the book and the letters were not a surprise. What shocked me was the encounter with things—real things—that had played a part in my life as a child. As a child, I pretended I was just like any other child in the Kibbutz by the Sea, except for the fact that I was waiting for my mother to come back from wherever she had gone. And my teachers pretended with me. Or perhaps it was my teachers who did the pretending and I pretended with them. That complicity of denial was destroyed by the arrival of our Bible teacher . . . .

---

*   see chapter notes

Fax to Miriam, 1997

Dear Miriam:

I have just sent a Power of Attorney and asked Mr. Marks to represent my outstanding claims from Germany, including the claim for Grandfather's house in Rosswein.

I am forwarding the enclosed material to you in the hope that you may reconsider your engagement with URO. Had I thought that Theuerkauf would *actively pursue* our claim, or, in any way do a better job then WM did, I would gladly have joined with you.

I contacted Theuerkauf shortly after your visit at least three times, trying to get answers to my question about the structure of his fees, and how we were to communicate, given that I do not speak or read German. All I have received in reply was a request for a power of attorney.

I had engaged Ms. Kelleher to provide us with an assessment of the prospects of *gaining possession of grandfathers house* at your prompting and approval. I have kept you informed of what she was doing, every step of the way.

I think I deserve an explanation as to why, after agreeing to go ahead with the assessment, you decided to have URO* represent your claim, before the result of the assessment was in. It is my impression that both Theuerkauf and WM provide the same nineteenth century dead-letter-box legal services, which I am afraid, will do us no good, if we want to repossess grandfather's house.

Let me know what you intend to do.

Peter

---

* United Restitution Organization

UNITED RESTITUTION ORGANIZATION (URO)

Sophienstrasse 26-60487 Frankfurt/M—Tel.: 069-970701-0—Fax:
069-970701-50—Telegramm-Adresse: Uroclaims Frankfurt

Frankfurt/M., 4. Mär 1997

Ihre Ansprüche nach dem VermG
Hier: Grundst*ü*ck in Roßwein, M*ü*hlstraße 18

Dear Mr. Paz:

We acknowledge with thanks receipt of your fax of Feb. 28th.
Answering your questions we should like to tell you that URO, a
non profit organization, operates on the basis of Success, that means,
URO receives 10 % of whatever you and the other heirs receive as
restitution. In case the value exceeds DM 1.000.000,—, the fees
is gradually reduced. We should like to ask you if you wish to be
represented by us, like your cousin, Mrs. Miriam London.

In this case, we ask you to sign and return to us the attached
form of power of attorney.

Hoping to have answered your questions.

Sincerely,
Herr Reeh

Fax from Miriam London, July 12, 1997

Hello Peter:

I have received notification from Landratsamt Dobeln that our claim for our grandfather's property in Rosswein was refused on the grounds that the current owner inherited the property from people who had purchased it from the person to whom Grandfather "sold" it. The court will determine final compensation for us.

Your wish to regain the property and develop it and this decision will devastate you. I sympathize with your pain. We all have an emotional attachment to the property and it is unfair that we are deprived of it.

It may be the most fortunate outcome for us though.

My mother's family also had a property and her brother and John and I are joint heirs. The court awarded the property to our family because the original "buyer" is still the owner. But it isn't so simple. The owner is now claiming enormous amounts of money for redevelopments he claims to have made. It is a nightmare and my mother's brother says that we would be best to walk away with nothing as the amounts being claimed plus legal fees will be higher than we could realize on the property.

All good wishes to you and Beverly.

Please keep in touch.

With love,
Miriam and Joe

Fax to Miriam London, December 26, 1997

Dear Miriam:

Sorry it has taken me so long to get back to you. Though the Landratsamt Dobeln's decision to award Grandfather's house to the Ginters was no surprise, I was stunned by the decision. I had hoped that the Landratsamt Dobeln would, at least, provide us with a comprehensible text, so we might, at least, understand our loss, or else fashion a meaningful response to their decision.

What we got from the Landratsamt Dobeln instead is a clumsy justification for their decision, replete with transparently self-serving declarations that "all was done legally!" A decision in legalese, including incomplete references to a law, supposedly proclaimed on May 8, 1945, the very day Nazi Germany collapsed, capitulated—a day when Rosswein, including Berlin, was occupied by Russian troops—a day when Germany, effectively, had no government.

A week before Christmas, I got a registered envelope from the Senatsverwaltung, the Berlin senate. I realized at first glance that it had to do with my German nationality and my German passport, which I got two years ago, after a seven-year campaign and three sets of lawyers. Enclosed also was a cover note from the German Vice Consul in Marseille, who signed her letter, the German old fashioned way, "Mit freundlichen Grusen, Iris Schirra."

When I told her on the phone that I did not speak German and, therefore, could not respond to her letter, she reverted to the new German way, saying: "There is nothing to understand, Mr. Paz! The German Senatsverwaltung in Berlin has stripped you of your German nationality. We want you to return your German passport and Certificate of German Nationality immediately!" She was speechless when I told her that I would not respond to her letter until I received a full and detailed English translation of the Senatsverwaltung document, which I am still waiting for.

The next morning, I woke up with a mental picture of myself (the one in a photo you brought of me) standing in the fifth position, between Grandmother and Grandfather. Looking at that image in my mind's eye, I had a flashback memory of myself sitting in the Landratsamt Dobeln, staring at Grandfather's handwriting in the ledger in front of me. There was no date of sale, but the year Grandfather "sold" the house to one Bruno Max Taubert was marked in the ledger as 1937.

THE PROBLEM WITH THE PHOTOS

The significance of the Rosswein photograph:

Since in the picture with Grandfather and Grandmother I am about three to four years old and *since I was born on the 31 of August 1937, that picture could not have been taken before 1940, possibly 1941*, long after Grandfather was reported to have been deported to Theresienstadt.

Conclusion:

The most reasonable explanation of the above is that Grandfather *actually* sold the property in 1940-1941, well after Kristallnacht,* and that the sale was deliberately backdated, possibly by Bruno Max Taubert, and/or by his widow.

The obvious motive for back-dating the date of the sale is that the sale of property by Jews to Germans *before* Kristallnacht was considered by Germans a legitimate, normal, commercial, legal transaction; whereas, *after* Khristalnacht such "sales" were considered confiscations.

We may not get Grandfather's house back but we may justly demand that the Landratsamt Dobeln, who declared that their ruling was based on facts and the law, produce a credible explanation for the following:

1) Alfons Goldmann's whereabouts, between the time he sold his property to Mr. Taubert in 1937 and 1940 /1941, and the time the said picture was taken.
2) The presence of Alfons Goldmann in Rosswein in 1940, at least 3 years after he was reported (by the Landratsamt Dobeln document) to have been deported to Theresienstadt.

The Bootger Schle report:

It seems that the Landratsamt Dobeln has overlooked material facts that were discovered by Bootger Schle, the German associates of the Australian lawyer Kelleher: These omissions raise questions about the legitimacy of the transaction between the Lofflers and the Ginters, with respect to the sale of the property by Hertha Loffler in 1974 to Erich and Johana Ginter, the parents of Peter Ginter.

---

* November 9-10, 1938

According to the Australian lawyer Kelleher, her associates in Germany, Botter, Schle, reported that the price Erich Ginter paid Hertha Loffler for the property in 1974, (thirty-seven years later) was some 60 per cent below* the price Bruno Max Taubert paid Grandfather for the property in 1937, a transaction considered by the Landratsamt Dobeln to have been a "forced sale."

Since the Kelleher information has a direct bearing on whether or not the sale by Hertha Loffler to the Ginters qualifies as a bona fide transaction based on the properties market value, URO may pose the question to Mr. Hertzog at the Landratsamt Dobeln.

I did pass on this information to WM and WM, assuming they would pass it along to Mr. Hertzog at the Landratsamt Dobeln.

There are a number of errors in the Landratsamt Dobeln as well as the URO documents: for instance, the document claiming that we are all children of Helen Goldmann, I am assuming the errors have been corrected.

As you recall, when I visited WM and JH in Berlin, WM showed me a copy of Grandfather's will in which he left half of the property to your father and half to my mother. Logically, I am due one-half the compensation as the sole heir of my mother and you and John will divide your father's share.

Much of the problem with our claim, as I see it, lies in the typically European aversion to providing fully detailed and comprehensible information, which effectively keeps us out of the process. That is why I favored an English-speaking lawyer to attend to our claim.

Being that I have been out of work for close to four years now. I am afraid that we will not be able to make it to Zoey's wedding. We are very sorry.

We both wish you joy and happiness.

Beverly and Peter

---

* Peter's reasoning was that the original (confiscated) price was so low that when the house was resold, even for a profit, the resale price was still way below market value.

FAX MESSAGE: URGENT

Attention: Theuerkauf
United Restitution Organization
Re: The Landratsamt's Dobeln decision with respect to the property
at 18, Muhlstrasse Rosswein

Dear Mr. Theuerkauf:

Enclosed please find the following:

Response to the The Landratsamt's Dobeln decision with respect to the property at 18, Muhlstrasse Rosswein

Evidence that calls into question the integrity of the *1937 date of sale* of the property at 18, Muhlstrasse, Rosswein by Alfons Goldmann to Bruno Max Taubert.

3 Photographs numbered # 1-2-3 . . . .

Editor's note: The rest of the content of this fax is identical to the information in the preceding fax to Miriam (see above), with the following addition:

I would also like you to investigate:

Alfons Goldmann's property Insurance policy.

Since the Properties File at the Landratsamt Dobeln registry listed Alfons Goldman as owner of 50 % of the property since 1901, see list below, and since the said property was a major store on one of Rosswein's main commercial streets, Alfons Goldmann, no doubt held insurance on the property.

It is unlikely that Alfons Goldmann would have continued to pay insurance for a property he had sold in 1937. A check with Alfons Goldman's insurance company may very well yield the answer as to when he actually sold the house to Bruno Max Taubert. The property's insurance file should also yield answers as to when Bruno Max Taubert took over the insurance payments for the property.

Alfons Goldmann's Life Insurance Policy.

Since the Rosswein photograph shows Alfons Goldmann alive and well in Rosswein in 1940/41, and since Alfons Goldman had a wife, two children, and two grandchildren to support, he surely had a life insurance policy.

The said policy must be considered as an inseparable part of Alfons Goldmann's estate, before the estate is probated.

A check with his life insurance company may also shed light on important, yet-unanswered questions.

In conclusion:

It is my belief that the Landratsamt's Dobeln decision with respect to the property at 18 *Muhlstrasse* Rosswein cannot be considered valid without considering the new evidence and the questions enclosed herein.

For your records: The house at 18 Muhlstrasse, Rosswein:

The property is 270 square meters. The front house is 3 stories high.

In the back there is another house that is two stories high and about 20x7 meters.

It has at least one tenant.

The front house is in very good condition and is fully occupied. It faces a street that is a mix of commercial and residential properties.

The ground floor is a plumber's workshop.

The upper-floors are rented. Ginter (the present owner) lives in the second floor apartment facing the street. The third floor seems to be rented to a party named Fuchs.

The registered owners of the house at 18 Muhlstrase:

1901: Alfons Goldmann owned 50% of the property.

1907: Alfons Goldmann owned 100% of the property.

1937-1945: Bruno Max Taubert

1945-1974: Taubert's widow, B. Seifert remarried a Mr. Loeffler and the property was registered under his name.

1974 The property was sold by Loffler to Erich & Johana Ginter on Feb. 20. 1974.

The house, although old, appears to be in perfect condition. Neither Rosswein nor Dobeln appear to have suffered any war damage.

Sincerely,
Peter Paz

CC.
Herzog at:
Landratsamt, Dobeln
Federal Republic of Germany
Postfach 7 und 8
04711 Dobeln

MIRIAM LONDON
FAX
DATE: May 28, 1998
TO: Peter Paz
FROM: Miriam London
RE: Landratsamt Dobeln
Number of pages including cover sheet: 1

Message

Dear Peter,

I hope all is well.

Another letter has come from the Landratsamt Dobeln.

They have asked me whether you want to sustain your objection to the decision of July 1997 to offer us monetary restitution or whether the possibility exists that you may withdraw your objection. I have written and told them that they should direct their enquiry to you, so you will probably hear from them in a week or so.

I hope your renovations are going according to plan.

With love,
Miriam

Fax to Miriam London, April 22,1999

Dear Miriam:

I am wondering why I haven't heard from you after I responded to your last fax in which you expressed concern that I may be blocking progress in resolving the final disposition of Grandfather's house. What exactly are you referring to?[*]

In my response to your last fax I did my very best to reassure you that to the best of my knowledge I have done nothing that in any way may impede progress in the resolution of Grandfather's house. The Germans have made known their decision not to respect our request to take possession of the house. However, as far as I know, the Germans have made no offer. Until an offer is made, I see no reason why we should not make every effort to regain possession of the house.

I have not sent the photographs to WM and HJ, because I have been unsuccessful in contacting them for over a year. But I did send the photograph and what I thought was significant about them to the parties concerned (see my fax dated 12/26/1997). I suggest you ask Theuerkauf what, if anything, he has done with the pictures. The photographs, after all, represent unassailable evidence that challenges the Doblen's Board's contention that Alfons Goldmann sold his property to Bruno Max Taubert in 1937.

I believe that a close look at the records will confirm that Grandfather did sell the house to Bruno Max Taubert, but that the sale took place in 1941 or 1942, as the photo suggests, and that to avoid having the property classified as a forced sale, the sale was backdated to 1937.

I believe we do have a real chance to regain Grandfather's house, but our only hope lies in us working together and making constructive use of our lawyers. Which means that, at the minimum,

---

[*] Peter refused to accept the principal of a monetary compensation for the house before knowing the amount the Germans intended to offer. Miriam thought this refusal was blocking the progress of the claim.

we must be provided with correspondence and documents in a language that we understand.

I look forward to hearing what you think.

Have been trying to get in touch with Goldi* and Myra. Has there been a change in their fax & email? Please send me a fax, with your present fax number.

My very best wishes,
Your cousin, Peter

P.S. I will be sending a copy of this fax to URO, provided I can I receive their correspondence/documents in English. I have, reluctantly, changed my mind and plan to ask Theuerkauf to represent me, since this may be the only way we can resolve this.

---

*   David, Miriam's brother

Fax to Miriam London, March 3, 2000

Dear Miriam:

I've wanted to write you for a long time about where we are in the process of getting compensation for Grandfather's house.

I received correspondence from Herzog from Dolbeln in German on June 2, 1999. Beverly insisted that we have it translated to expedite the process, so we did. In that letter, they said it was impossible to return the property for, in my opinion, not very good reasons. I had hoped that they would respond to my previous letter in which I pointed out that the house was sold to the Ginters in 1974 for 60 percent less than the Tauberts paid in 1937, and that they paid only 3000DM. (This was the finding of the Australian lawyer that you recommended we contact.) I also alerted Herzog to the fact that the date of the original sale of 1938 to Taubert had been falsified. The proof of this is that I have a picture of me with my grandparents at age of three to four at the house. I was born in 1937. However, Herzog's letter did not address any of these issues.

I subsequently responded to Herzog in English, August 2, 1999, with some new information, namely that they underestimated the size of the property by at least 600 square meters. *I concluded the letter, however, saying that I would be willing to accept compensation if they let us know in advance the amount.** I also requested that they send all future correspondence in English. I never got a response to that letter until a few days ago, when I received a one-page letter from Dresden in English saying that they were legally bound to transmit all legal decisions in German. They required that I have a representative in Germany to accept their correspondence.

When Beverly was in Berlin last February, she tried to contact WM's office but there was no answer. She called again this week and got a new number and actually got to speak to HJ on the phone.

---

*   It was, Peter said, a "Catch 22," since the Germans would not reveal the amount until Peter agreed to accept the payment.

He said that as far as he knows, he can do nothing more to help us, but requested that we send the latest communications to him. He said that he would be able to receive their correspondence and send it on to me with the gist of it translated.

I think that you might be required to agree with me that we will accept compensation if they let us know the amount in advance. Are you willing to agree to this? I know that you are as eager as I am to get this resolved, but we must not let them "get us out of the way" with an insultingly low compensation.

Hope all else is well with you and the kids. I had a particularly rough winter and had pneumonia again, which I am still getting over.

Love,
Peter

Fax to Peter from Miriam London, April 3, 2000

Dear Peter,

I had a thought after sending you the fax on 31 March.

As I have already told you, John and I have accepted the court's decision of 16/07/97 awarding us monetary compensation for the forced sale of our grandfather's property in Rosswein.

Because you protested against the decision and have not withdrawn your protest, your protest has now been lodged with another court which will decide in the fullness of time, whether or not to uphold your protest. You have every right to protest, even though I do not agree with you.

If the court decides not to uphold your protest, then I assume that our case will return to its previous course, and that we will be granted monetary compensation by decision of the Treasury . . . eventually.

There is nothing that either John or I can do at this stage.

If you wish to withdraw your protest you can try to do that. It may be possible.

Beverly's experiences with HJ are interesting. As I have told you, my own experiences of HJ are less favorable and there is no way that I would enlist his services again.

My involvement with this claim has forced me to translate all the documents and caused me the onerous task of writing letters in German.

I have absolutely no intention at this stage to engage a translator or a legal representative. Beverly has a good command of German. She mentioned that she has lived there and I think that she could tell you the gist of any correspondence.

As I have said, I think that there is no action available to us just now other than if you wish to try to withdraw your protest.

Zoey's baby has not come yet. It is due 8 April. I will let you know when it arrives.

With good wishes, Miriam

X

Fax to Miriam London, September 2000

Dear Miriam:

I did receive your fax, but Beverly's son was here from Alaska
and I wanted to have time to think about it. When I received the
document, I called HJ, who advised me not to contest the decision.
"We don't have time or money to investigate your claim," he said,
and he doesn't think anything will change their decision. HJ said
that, at this point, we should accept the settlement and that is
what I am going to do. He said that there are fairly standard legal
appraisals of the property and the amount of our settlement should
be twenty percent of its worth. I think it is the best we can do, and
we should not drag this out any further. I would like to close this
chapter of my life.

However, Beverly found an organization in the U.S. for
processing insurance claims. I want to pursue this as I believe that
Grandfather must have had insurance on the property. I am sending
you the information and Beverly will fill out the papers for us. But
I need to know the spelling of Grandmother's maiden name and,
if possible, the date she left Germany and when she died.

We are as well as can be expected at this age.

Regards to you all,

I look forward to your response.

Love, Peter

Fax to Peter from Miriam London, January 5, 2001

Dear Peter:

Please forgive me for taking so long to reply to your last fax.

I'm glad that you have decided to move on in regard to our German claim. It is probably the wisest choice.

The decision by the Sachaiches Landesamt not to uphold your appeal was logical and expected . . . Now we must await the decision on the financial restitution. I hope they will award us more than the 20% of the value of the property as you told me HJ had suggested. We have an opportunity to appeal if we disagree with their offer.

Thank you for faxing me the forms (the insurance claim). It reminded me that I also have forms . . . I had set them aside to attend to when I retire . . . and now that time has come.

Grandma's maiden name was Griesbach. I can't tell you the date she left Germany, but I think it was about 1948 or 1949. She died in 1952.

I'll close with good wishes to you and Beverly for the New Year.

With love,
Miriam

*   *   *

Peter had another bout of pneumonia in the winter of 2001 from which he never completely recovered. He was subsequently diagnosed with spheroocytosis, a disease of the red blood cells, and was operated on in May to remove his spleen.

In August 2001, Peter received notification that he would be getting the equivalent of $7,000.00 as his share of the compensation for his grandfather's house. He said he was relieved that "the page was turned." Though disappointed at the small amount, he said, "It will be enough for us to take a vacation." But there was no time left for a vacation. Peter had a relapse in September and, after another month of hospitalization, died at home in Nice on October 21, 2001.

In 2003, his daughter, Lyrissa, received Peter's share for the house in Rosswein. The amount, surprisingly, turned out to be larger than had been offered. She is still pursuing the insurance claims.

EPILOGUE

—from Rex Ruthman's condolence letter to Beverly Pimsleur, read at the service for Peter in Nice, where he was buried at sea, as he had requested.

These are times when what we know must come, but never believe, does come. How sad, that still within the reach of our youths we have become the survivors of so many human histories already completed.

I will always remember Peter's unfailing grace in the face of disappointment and frustration, his kindness in a world that was not kind, and his passionate care about the things he found interesting, which made him always interesting in turn.

This summer he was obviously frail and confused, but he was never weak and never submissive. Now we learn—again—how the irreplaceable qualities of people emerge—most often in their absence.

Sadness of this kind forces wisdom or we cannot go on.

CHAPTER NOTES

Title: "The Forgetting of Being" was Peter's title for his memoir. It is a quote from the work of the German philosopher, Martin Heidegger, 1889-1976, a pupil of Edmund Husserl, 1859-1938, to whom the quote has also been attributed. (For origin of quote, see *The Art of the Novel* by Milan Kundera, Harper Collins, 2003)

About the Author: The name Paz: It is not clear where the name Paz originated. It might have been given to Peter on the kibbutz when they replaced his first name with Yigal, since "paz" means gold in Hebrew. In the legal records from Peter's lawyer, WM, sent to Peter's daughter Lyrissa after Peter's death, it is indicated that Peter's father was named Leo Rubenfeld and that Dorthea Goldmann was unwed at the time of Peter's birth. Peter thought this might have explained why his mother's brother, Rudolf, did not attempt to get him and his mother out of Germany to Australia. But this could not be verified.

In 1961, the kibbutz sent Peter to Haifa to learn some new folk dances for its annual Pesach celebration. As a result of these classes, Peter joined a folk dance group that performed in Europe. This eventually led to his meeting the American choreographer Anna Sokolov and his career in dance.

After Peter quit dance, he tried his hand at various jobs before devoting himself full-time to photography. Along with his wife Luba Paz, he began shooting on assignment. He told Beverly that Luba taught him everything he knew about color photography.

CHAPTER 1: Peter's maternal grandmother was not Jewish and was able to live until the end of the war in Germany. She emigrated soon after the war to Australia and lived with her son Rudolf and his family until her death in the early 1950s.

CHAPTER 2: Goldberg Commission: In 1981 *The American Jewish Commission on the Holocaust* was established, chaired by former Supreme Court Justice Arthur J. Goldberg. The commission set out "to record and publish the truth . . . as to what American Jewish leaders did, and what indeed they might have been able to do in all of the circumstances to mitigate the massive evils of the Holocaust."

CHAPTER 4: Peter's grandfather's house was located in the town of Rosswein, 144 miles due south of Berlin, formerly in East Germany, It was the unification of Germany that made it possible for Peter to visit the property. Peter refers to the house in Rosswein as "the house he was born in," but he was, in fact, born in Berlin.

CHAPTER 5: The letters: It is not certain how many letters to Joe, Lyrissa, and friends were actually sent, but probably not as many as are reproduced in the manuscript (MS). It was perhaps a device that enabled Peter to write. Or perhaps he intended, but never got around to, sending all of the letters. They are dated where dates exist for them.

CHAPTER 6: Peter lived in Tel Aviv where he studied dance for a year before leaving for the United States.

CHAPTER 9: The letters that Miriam brought with her were from Peter's mother, Dorthea, written to her mother, Magdalena, and to Peter from her prison cell. In them, she refers to the fact that she went through Peter's birth entirely alone and implies that Peter's grandparents did not even know of Peter's existence until he was three years old. She tells her mother that is why it is so hard to be separated from her son, who she cared for alone and to whom she was so close. It is not clear where Peter was at this time, although it seems that he was in the care of his grandmother for a part of the period that his mother was in prison.

One last letter in August 1944 was from Ravensbruck, where Dorthea died a few months later. It reflects her anxiety and desperation about her ability to survive the harsh camp conditions and her concern for her mother, who was in ill health, and for Peter's safety. In her attempt to save him, she recommends that her mother try to place him in a Carolinenstift, at that time, a religiously run children's home, and to have him converted, because, she writes, "I wanted to raise him Protestant like I am myself."

According to Dorthea's letters, Peter was placed temporarily in one of these schools, possibly in Berlin, and though it is not clear where Peter was when he was deported, it is likely that it was from one of these schools. Peter did not remember the name of the concentration camp in which he was interned, but he did remember that it was liberated by the Russians at the end of the war.

Peter did not have his mother's letters translated during his lifetime, as it was probably too emotionally painful. The irony is that the reader now knows more about Peter's life than he did, due to the information discovered in the letters and the research done by Marianne Salinger of the Baeck Institute.

The originals of Dorthea Goldmann's letters and the voluminous correspondence between Peter and the various German agencies (and their responses in German) are available for consultation at the Leo Baeck Institute, Fifteen West Sixteenth Street, NY, New York.

ACKNOWLEDGEMENTS

Everyone who knew Peter thought he had a story to tell and were waiting for him to finish the "memoirs," someday. I had read the text as it evolved and was eager to see it completed and eventually published. In the last few years of Peter's life, his frustrating struggle to reclaim his citizenship and his grandfather's house, his despair about the Intifada and his illness, disheartened him from writing and wore him down. But a few months before he died, he told me that he wanted to go back to work on his book and to include the letters about his attempts to reclaim his grandfather's house. However, he never recovered sufficiently to work on the book again. His friends encouraged me to undertake the unfinished task of assembling his writings into something publishable, out of love for him and as a record for his daughter, Lyrissa.

Without all those who supported me, I never would have had the courage to complete this, but it ultimately helped me to live through the years after his death and, in the presence of his words, remind me of what I always knew, but sometimes forgot: that he was unique in every way and that, though never easy, he enriched my life with his, as he did for all who had the privilege to know him.

To our friends who helped me: Ralph Setton, who generously gave of his time to resolve many of the computer problems of transferring Peter's texts from various programs; Stan Goldberg, our New York friend and "tech" support who was Peter's computer "guru," helping him in various projects, always graciously; my cousins, Sheila Malovany-Chevallier and Bill Chevallier, who shared my sorrows and helped me in the first stages of dealing with the mass of manuscript material; Louis Chaclis and Francoise Galzin, who helped me through my discouraged moments; Elizabeth and Rex Ruthman and her mother Madame Busittil, who cared about and cared for Peter; Lyrissa and Luba Paz, who became more of my family than ever while I tried to complete this work; my children, Julia and Marc-Andrew, who allowed me to appropriate their offices to work in before I had one of my own, and who probably heard more about this manuscript than they cared to, but never complained; the Leo Baeck Institute: Dr. Mecklenburg, Viola Voss, the very helpful archivist, and Marianne Salinger, for her caring translation of Dorthea Goldmann's letters and for her research to find more information about Dorthea's and Peter's life during the war years.

To those friends who volunteered to read the manuscript as it progressed: Larry and Rochelle Sullivan, the first readers of Peter's partial MS who encouraged me to wrest the remainder of it from his computer; William Colby, who urged me to bring the MS to completion; Elaine Sloan, my loyal and supportive friend, for her encouragement to continue; Dan Rous, who read the MS with meticulous attention; Paula Glatzer for initial copy editing help; Kathy Bunin, invaluable for her many contributions; Karen Chervin for her empathy and insightful comments; Lanie Goodman, my loyal friend, for being there for me through it all; my cousin and friend, Melanie Fleishman, whose editorial help was invaluable at all stages of the MS and whose welcoming home in Sag Harbor gave me the peace of mind to begin the task of putting together Peter's book; a special thanks to Luba Paz, who took on the heroic task of copy editing the completed manuscript—the final edit is indebted to her "sharp eyes"; to Jane Assimacopoulos, for the last pass over the entire MS; to my dear niece, Adrienne Ruud—writer, poet, friend—who helped resolve some final editorial problems and to my English cousin, Audrey Jones, who provided the last, but not the least of the valuable editorial suggestions.

Family and friends, thank you all.

Beverly Pimsleur
New York, 2005

Roswein, 1938

Dorthea Goldmann's, Peter's
mother

Peter* with grandparents, Alfons
and Magdalena Goldmann,
Roswein, c. 1940

Peter, c. 1940

Peter (right) Esther Katzenelsen and her Son c. 1946

Roswein 1990

Peter in front of 18, Muhistrasse, 1990

Cousin Miriam, Beverly and Peter, Nice, 1995

Peter and Beverly in Nice apartment 1992

Luba and Lyrissa Paz, c. 1981

Lyrissa Paz, 2007

Peter Paz, photographer
1937-2001